Carving Wild Animals

Life-Size Wood Figures

Carving Wild Animals

Life-Size Wood Figures

Bill Dehos &
Patrick Spielman

Sterling Publishing Co., Inc.   New York

The authors extend a thank-you to the Peter Charles and the Childs families for allowing us to photograph the bear cub and the howling wolf from their personal collections. We also extend our appreciation to Mary Leisk, for her research on animal descriptions and behaviors. Julie Kiehnau's efficient and speedy typing is once more immensely appreciated.

Library of Congress Cataloging-in-Publication Data

Dehos, Bill.
    Carving wild animals : life-size wood figures / Bill Dehos and
Patrick Spielman.
       p.   cm.
    Includes index.
    ISBN 0-8069-6732-3 (pbk.)
    1. Wood-carving—Patterns.   2. Animal sculpture. I. Spielman,
Patrick E. II. Title.
TT199.7.D44   1988
731.4'62—dc19   88-12322
                                            CIP

CONTENTS

INTRODUCTION

Carving Wild Animals is a companion volume to the popular book, Carving Large Birds (Sterling Publishing Co., Inc., N.Y., 1986). The format or style and the techniques presented in these books are similar. The carving subjects themselves are the major differences. This book provides over 20 life-size carving projects of well-known North American wild animals.

As in carving the larger bird species in their full size, carving life-sized wild animals is exceptionally satisfying and enjoyable. This activity is likely to be a new or different and somewhat challenging experience for most wood carvers. Not many wood carvers would normally attempt such sculptures for fear of the unknown. This book will attempt to strip away such reasons, or excuses, for avoiding this seemingly awesome and difficult carving experience.

Carving Wild Animals presents a wide variety of animals in different size ranges, from a small red squirrel to a life-size cougar that's nearly 7 feet in overall length. Every wild-animal carving is interesting and affords a certain degree of challenge. The carver who wants to do a large animal will find the procedures basic and systematic leading to an end result that is highly impressive with a reward well worth the effort.

For many of the carvings, the logical and most practical beginning is cutting the log and "roughing it out" with a chain saw. The excitement grows as the shape continues to emerge from the crude log form. This sort of carving also offers its rewards in terms of pure physical, fresh-air exercise. Much of the carving can be performed at the material source, in the woodlot, out-of-doors and close to nature.

The carver will experience techniques and instruction for achieving the general recognizable shape of the animal. The objective need not be to reproduce every conceivable and minute detail. Techniques and instructions devoted to achieving special individual and generally recognizable features of animals are included. Special sections show how to make the eyes, nose, claws or feet, tails, and so on, of various animals. You'll find that most of the techniques are essentially the same for each category.

The methods are simple and straightforward. Slight changes in size, pose, behavior, color, or overall general effect will match the detail correctly to the animal being carved. For example, the tooling techniques and methods involved to carve and detail a rabbit ear might also be applied to carve and detail the ear of a fawn or other animal. Only the size, pose, and some shape differences taken from the drawings need to be identified and executed.

The instructions and carving examples show how to emphasize certain special features that are often common to more than one animal. Using the burning tool to color a claw or eye and to simulate individual hairs are easy techniques to master. The use of bleach to make a familiar light streak as in a skunk or to totally lighten a carving such as that of a snowshoe rabbit are other examples of simple but highly effective techniques that complement the truly natural effect afforded by massive carvings of solid woods.

Emphasis is almost always on the natural features of the wood itself. You will see how cracks can often add interest and age to a carving rather than be a detraction or a fresh-looking defect. In keeping with this concept, you'll see how to carve eyes so that no glass or plastic eyes need to be used that might visually cheapen the work. Essentially, all the wood carvings are completed with natural finishes. Very few pigmented or transparent stains are used. We rely heavily on the inherent natural beauty and figure of the wood itself to be its own showcase rather than use colorful pigmented paints and enamels that hide rather than enhance the wood.

Each carving project is accompanied by multiview photos and drawings. Some have important techniques shown with clear, closeup photography to make it easier for the carver to duplicate that particular carving.

Once your first carving is completed, the creative juices will flow and other carvings will come in quick succession. You have plenty of choices to satisfy your adrenaline, including a sneaky fox stalking its prey or a different fox pose of being curled up in the sun and sleeping on a stump.

An adorable fawn done in decoy fashion is sure to delight everyone who carves it and those who will eventually view it. A hungry beaver gnawing at a stick or a cute little bear cub climbing a dead tree are other great sculptures done in their natural poses.

More naturalistic poses include the cougar shown with his legs curled ready to pounce on an unsuspecting victim, which is one of the most dramatic of the sculptures shown; the wolf howling at the moon or calling its mate is another of the action-type carvings. Alternatives to these bigger and more challenging carved sculptures are smaller ones recommended for the beginner. Easier carvings and those that require less material include a small squirrel, a weasel, a skunk, a snowshoe, and an alert mink.

Whatever your choice or the amount of your effort, the results are certain to be dramatic and worthwhile.

1
TOOLS AND BASIC TECHNIQUES

The animals illustrated in this book were carved with just a few basic tools. Although not all of those illustrated are absolutely necessary, you will find their use advantageous in terms of convenience and time saving, because large quantities of wood need to be removed when carving many of the large animals.

A chain saw, Illus. 1, is practically a necessity if you intend to cut up trees for your material. A lot of stock can be removed quickly with the chain saw during the early, roughing-out stages of producing a carving. The use of a chain saw is illustrated frequently throughout the book. However, handsaws and chisels or other power tools can be used for roughing out the carvings if so desired. The primary advantage of using a chain saw to rough out carvings is simply speed and convenience, because we already own several types of chain saws.

Illus. 1. A gas-type saw has adequate power for deep plunge and separation carving as shown here. Suggestion: Roughing out large carvings in the woodlot reduces their weight and bulk for greater ease in transporting.

A small, inexpensive electric chain saw, as shown in Illus. 2, is available at most hardware dealers. This offers the advantage of convenience in maneuverability and handling because of its light weight when compared to the heavier gas-powered chain saws. Other advantages of electric chain saws are: 1) You can start and stop easily by using the trigger switch. 2) They are good for indoor use because of their lack of exhaust smoke. 3) They are easier on the ears—they run more quietly than gas-engine saws. Manufacturers are also changing the design of saws and the cutting chains to improve their overall safety. However, if you're a novice, it would be prudent to get some personal, hands-on safety instruction from some knowledgeable individual, such as a chain-saw dealer or experienced logger. Always study and observe the manufacturer's safety recommendations for not only chain saws, but all other hand and power tools as well.

Illus. 2. The electric chain saw is inexpensive, lightweight, and ideal for indoor work.

One safety feature of chain saws that is well worth investigating is a newer style of chain designed to minimize kickback or bucking tendencies, which can be very dangerous with a chain saw. See Illus. 3. A

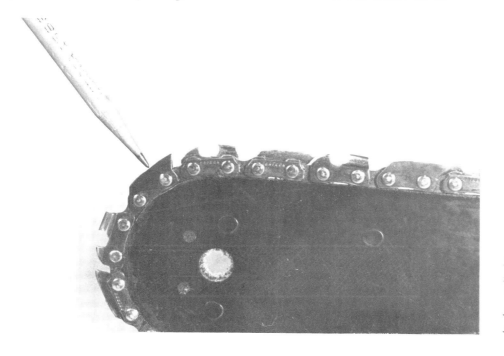

Illus. 3. A chain designed to minimize kickback or bucking. This has a "guard link" that is believed to be safer than the standard saw chain shown in Illus. 4.

Illus. 4. A close look at a standard saw chain.

standard chain is shown in Illus. 4 for a visual comparison. Notice the guard-link design, in Illus. 3, which tips out as the chain travels around the end of the bar. This reduces or controls the amount of bite when cutting with this area of the bar.

If desired, you might want to consider modifying the end of a standard chain-saw bar so that it has a sharper curve which permits cutting finer details than otherwise possible. See Illus. 5. Also, check with your chain-saw dealer about the availability of a special, narrow bar designed for chain-saw carving. One such type is a 12-inch size called a "carving bar." It is not illustrated here.

Illus. 5. Two chain-saw bars: The one in the foreground was ground to a sharper radius, making it more suitable for finer detailing. Be sure to grind the edge square; do not grind so deep that the drive tangs ride on the bottom of the channel.

Illus. 6 shows a new, experimental usage of saw chain for carving. As far as we know this tool is not currently available on the market. However, larger diameter blades similar to this and designed for use in table saws are available commercially. Turn to pages 80, 105, and 158 for just a few of the illustrations included in this book that show roughing-out work with the chain saw.

Illus. 6. Another application of the saw chain: This new, experimental tool cuts fast, but is somewhat difficult to control for precise work.

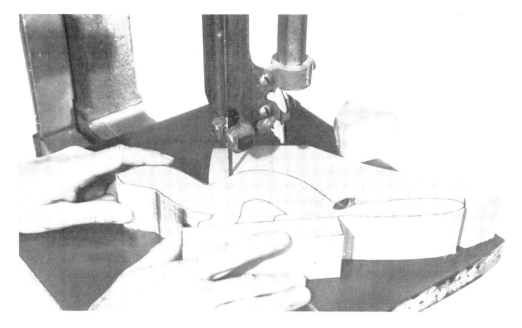

Illus. 7. The band saw is a useful device for roughing out certain carvings, particularly those made from dry wood and that have one surface prepared flat to rest on the saw table.

A *band saw*, Illus. 7, is certainly a timesaving piece of equipment, although it is expensive. Band saws are especially good for cutting laminated stock because it is usually dry wood and it has at least one flat surface. In preparing stock for laminating, jointers, planers, other saws, clamps, and so on, are sometimes required or at least helpful. The band saw is useful for roughing out some of the smaller animal carvings in this book.

A *die grinder*, Illus. 8, or some other powerful rotary tool is extremely useful and a practical consideration for the serious carver. The one shown in the photo rotates at 25,000 rpm and it will accept various cutters and burrs that have ¼-inch-diameter round shanks. The die grinder can be a roughing and a finishing tool with the appropriate cutters. It can be used to make various surface textures such as carved fur and simulated bark as shown in Illus. 9 and 10. Most surfaces can be shaped with this power tool, but the smooth flowing surfaces of beautiful woods require extra sanding to achieve a finish worthy of the carving.

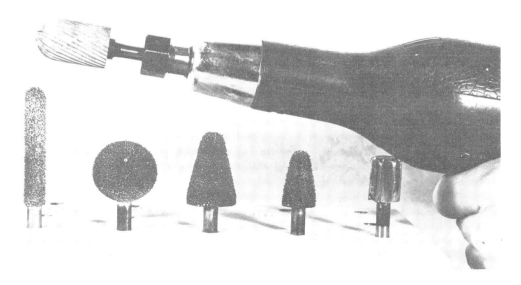

Illus. 8. A ¼" high-speed die grinder is extremely useful.

Illus. 8–10 show some steel and carbide cutters or burrs. Illus. 11 illustrates a typical set of steel cutting burrs. The structured carbide cutters (Illus. 8, 9, and 12) are ideal for working in tight areas, on burls, and so on. You do not have to always be concerned about cutting "with-the-grain" when using such cutters, as you need to be when using knives, chisels, and gouges. See Illus. 13 and 14. The structured carbide bits are available in many cutting shapes and in either ¼" or ⅛" shank sizes. See Illus. 15 and 16.

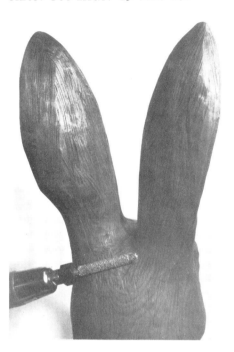

Illus. 9. Leaving some tool marks such as those made by this structured carbide burr simulates a hair or furlike texture.

Illus. 10. Using the end corner of a rotary tool to make V-grooves that help to simulate bark on the base of a carving.

Illus. 11. Steel cutting burrs are also available in many cutting profiles and they are available with a choice of shank sizes.

Illus. 12. Carbide burrs are available in various cutting grades, ranging from extra coarse (comparable to a 16-grit abrasive) to fine (comparable to a 60- or 80-grit abrasive).

Illus. 13. An example of the capabilities afforded by the structured carbide rotary cutters. This carving in its entirety was formed, shaped, and finally textured, all with the same tooling; that is, without any knife-cutting or sanding whatsoever.

Illus. 14. Right: A close-up showing the tooth structure of carbide burrs. This design permits a cool and fast cutting rate without loading or "gumming" up. These sharp tungsten carbide teeth are brazed to a steel body.

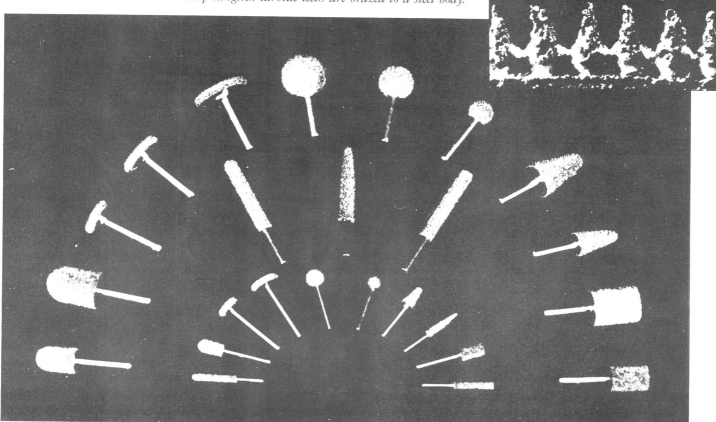

Illus. 15. Carbide burrs are available in various shapes and with a choice of ⅛" or ¼" shanks.

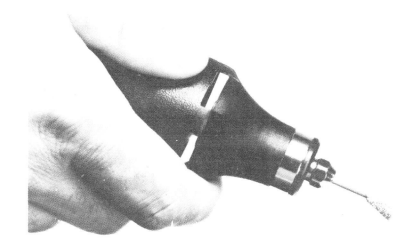

Illus. 16. A ³⁄₈" diameter dovetail-shaped cutter on a ¹⁄₈" diameter shank is ideal for detailing.

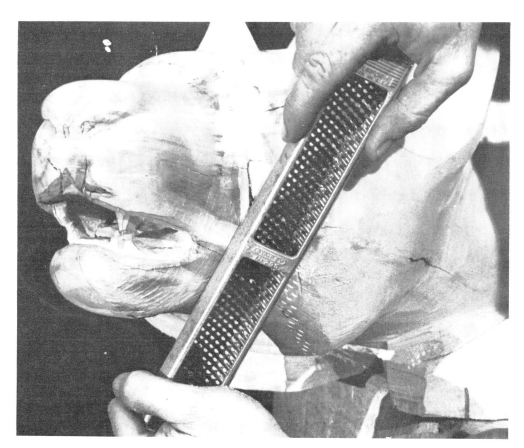

Illus. 17. The Surform® tool cuts and smooths. This tool is available in flat, half-round, round configurations as well as a drum type for use in a power drill.

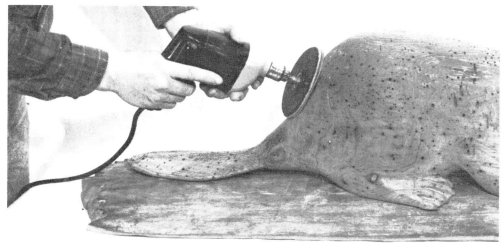

Illus. 18. A disc sander attachment for the electric drill is useful for smoothing and fairing a convex body line.

Files and rasps are also used to hand-shape and detail carvings. One popular type is the Surform® file shown in Illus. 17.

Power sanders, Illus. 18, are other convenience tools. You can always sand by hand! Carving smooth animals always requires some hand-sanding in "tight areas" anyway. So, when convex or other surfaces are conducive to power-sanding, time and "elbow grease" will be saved. It should be noted, too, that sanders are used to do much more than just smooth. It would be reasonable to say that sanders are used about equally for final shaping as well as for initial smoothing. The disc sanders are used to smooth out the rough surfaces made from chain-sawing, Illus. 18, and some of the surfaces worked with the die grinder. The larger disc sander in Illus. 19 carries a very coarse abrasive 36–50 grit and the drill attachment (shown in the same photo) carries an 80- or 100-grit abrasive. The circular sanding marks left from the disc sanders are taken out with the small pad sander and by hand. Small mounted sanding sleeves for use with a die grinder are available as shown in Illus. 20. These are extremely helpful when smoothing inside curves and various details. They work best when operated at slower speeds, that is, when the normal rpm is reduced with the use of a speed-control device. Otherwise, these sanding sleeves tend to load up and burn when used at high speeds.

Illus. 19. Power sanders: The large coarse disc on the right is ideal for use after the chain saw. Use it to simultaneously smooth while defining final contour shapes.

Illus. 20. Sanding sleeves on rubber-mounted shanks are also available in various shapes and in different abrasive grits.

Hand edge tools, Illus. 21–23, consist of carving chisels, gouges, carving knives, and whatever other types of edge tools you are comfortable with.

The tool sets shown in Illus. 21 and 22 are just suggestions, but fairly essential ones in our opinion. Many of the carvings in this book can be completed without all of these tools.

Illus. 21. Some basic carving tools: Small sizes at left, conventional full-sized carving tools at right, plus a mallet above and a knife made from an old straight razor, below at left.

Illus. 22. Some special carving chisels: The two at left are a large and a small spoon-shaped V-parting tool; and others are spoon gouges.

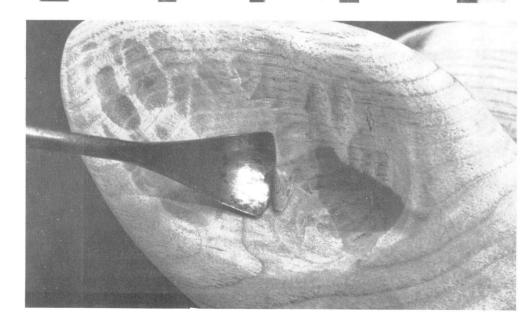

Illus. 23. Gouges come in all sizes and shapes and are used for many different tasks. Only a few well-chosen ones will handle a great number of different carving situations.

Carving knives, Illus. 24–26, are an area of possible controversy that we don't want to get too deeply into. Today, there are literally hundreds of different blade and handle configurations available for carvers to choose from. Use what suits your taste and experience best. Illus. 25 and 26 illustrate and discuss the possibility of actually making your own carving knives. Be very careful when grinding. Work slowly and do not overheat the steel. Final grinding can be done with a small disc sander/grinder rotating slowly on an electric hand drill. Polish with emery cloth.

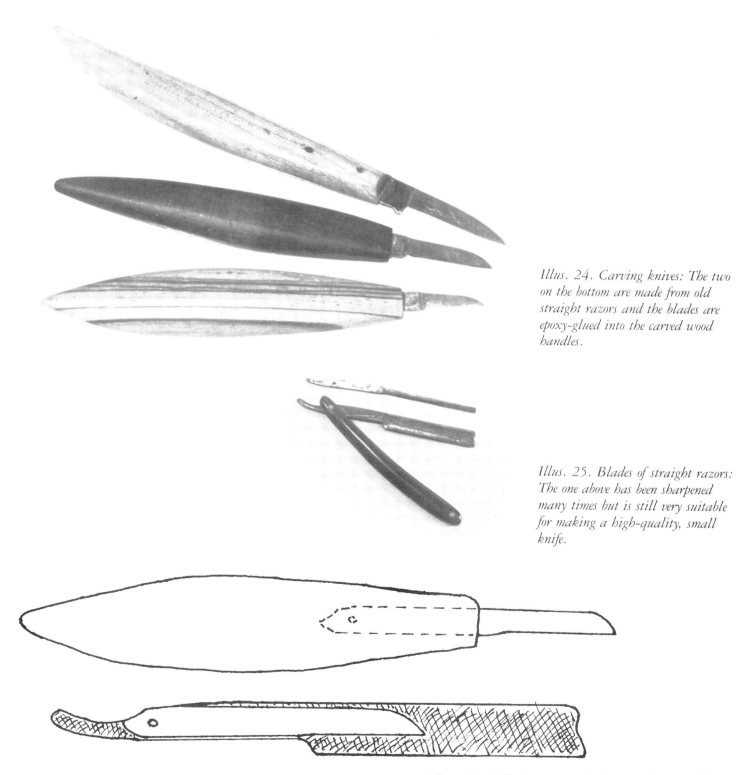

Illus. 24. Carving knives: The two on the bottom are made from old straight razors and the blades are epoxy-glued into the carved wood handles.

Illus. 25. Blades of straight razors: The one above has been sharpened many times but is still very suitable for making a high-quality, small knife.

Illus. 26. Full-size patterns for homemade carving knives.

A *woodburning tool*, Illus. 27, is very useful. Use it to deepen and darken lines in outlining details, to shade the pupils of eyes, or for shading areas such as the surfaces of an animal's claws, nose, and for making hair textures. See Illus. 28. Turn to page 199 which shows how the burning tool was used to sign the carving.

Other tools used to make the animals in this book include hand or electric drills, clamps, and vises, and some very special tools designed and made by author Dehos for forming carved eyes.

Illus. 27. A typical woodburning tool is especially useful for accenting various details and coloring.

Illus. 28. Woodburning the individual hairs, as shown here, also creates an interesting furlike look. The same woodburning tool is also useful to detail other features on many different carvings.

Eye-forming tools, Illus. 29 to 32, are easy to make and they are ideal for the beginning carver. Simply cut a length of mild steel rod from two to four inches in length. The diameters of the rod should equal the desired eye size. With a regular high-speed steel drill of the same diameter, drill into the end of the rod on its center as accurately as possible. See Illus. 29.

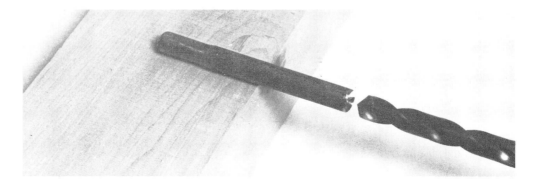

Illus. 29. Making eye-forming tools is easy. Simply drill into the end of mild steel rod, as shown here.

Drill only to a depth that produces a sharp rim around the end of the steel rod. Use a triangular file as shown in Illus. 30, and make a cutting lip for chip removal. Eye-forming tools of any size (Illus. 31) can be made in this manner. A fairly complete set includes: ¼ inch, ⁵⁄₁₆ inch, ⅜ inch, ⁷⁄₁₆ inch, ½ inch, ⁹⁄₁₆ inch, ⅝ inch, and ¾ inch sizes. They will form the eyes in this book with the exception of some totally hand-carved eyes. However, the forming tools can be used to define the pupils of these eyes as well. Illus. 32 is a good example of an eye.

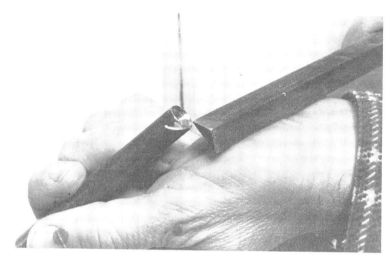

Illus. 30. To complete the eye-forming tool, file a "lip," as shown, with a triangular file.

Illus. 31. These eye-forming tools of various diameters are homemade from steel rods.

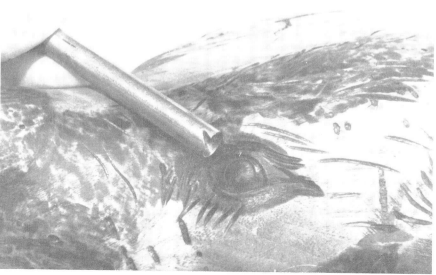

Illus. 32. The eye-forming tool is turned with a hand drill. Here it is used to form the eye of the badger carving. A slower rpm is preferable when using this tool.

Carving Eyes

Carving the eyes into the head is a whole lot easier than it looks. The homemade tools almost make eye-carving a "snap." See Illus. 33A-L. Carved eyes are preferred to the glass inserted eyes that are commonly used in decoy carving. Carved eyes appear much more artistic, and are in keeping with the integrity of a sculpted wood carving. In short, they are not so artificial looking, but appear more natural.

First, carve the eye area so it conforms to the general contour of the head, as shown in Illus. 33A. The large eyes of some animals are easy to carve with a knife and gouge. See Illus. 33B and 33E. If carving is of wormy wood, simplify the details, as shown in Illus. 33L. The surfaces of the pupil can be shaded. Carefully work the woodburning tool over the appropriate areas of the pupil to achieve a very alive, realistic look. Illus. 33H shows that the entire surface *is not* shaded. Eyeballs are not always perfectly round. Do not try for perfection. It's the effect that's important, not the accuracy or precise proportion.

Illus. 33. A study and examples of carved eyes: (A) snowshoe, (B) fawn, (C) fawn, (D) raccoon, (E) fox squirrel, (F) badger, (G) fox, (H) snowshoe, (I) bear, (J) jack rabbit, (K) wolf, and (L) howling wolf.

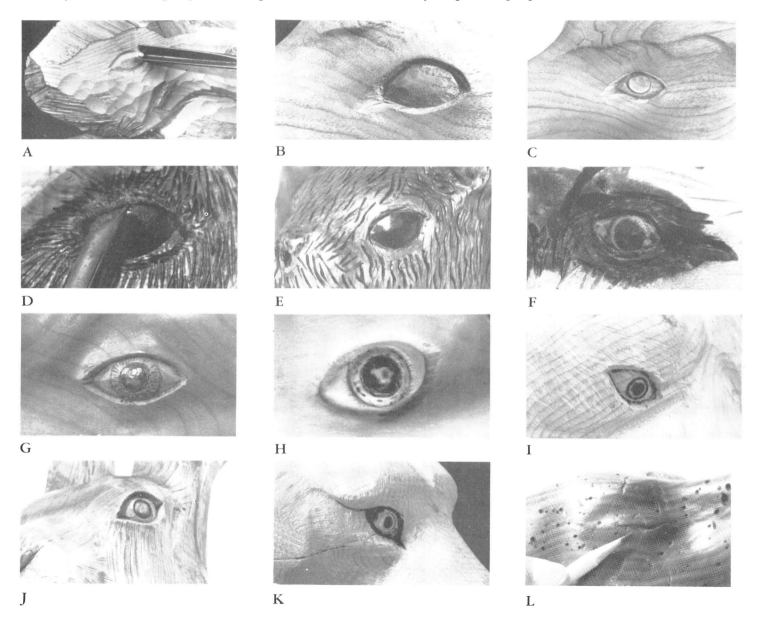

Bases and Feet

It is essential for some carvings that the animal be standing or effectively supported on a base. See Illus. 34–36. Almost every carving with a base is made with the animal and base carved from one piece. The roughing-out operation is very important and it's much like planning and making two carvings in one. Illus 36–38 graphically illustrate animal carvings with integral bases. Feet and claws are carved simultaneously with the base so that all the details come together effectively.

Illus. 34. Bases can be attached to the carving or made to be an integral one-piece work as the example on the left.

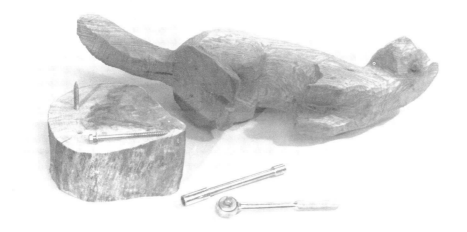

Illus. 35. A base of a different wood than the carving sometimes adds more character. Another reason for having a base is to protect delicately carved claws and toes.

Illus. 36. Here's a one-piece carving. The visual separation of the body and base is achieved by staining one differently than the other.

Illus. 37. Undercutting contributes to the visual separation of the animal and its integral base. Contrasting stains take this a step further.

Illus. 38. An example of a one-piece base and carving. This base is carved to resemble an old weathered tree or stump.

Preliminary roughing of the feet or claws begins with a gouge or chisel. Illus. 39A and 39B show the shape starting to develop. The woodburning tool can be, again, an effective tool used in shading the surfaces of the claws. Illus. 39C. Some other techniques and examples of animal feet are shown in Illus. 39D to 39F. Some carvings themselves or those having big, thick, or massive bases should be hollowed out to reduce bulk and reduce weight. See Illus. 314 on page 184. Hollowing relieves stresses, speeds drying, and minimizes checking and cracking.

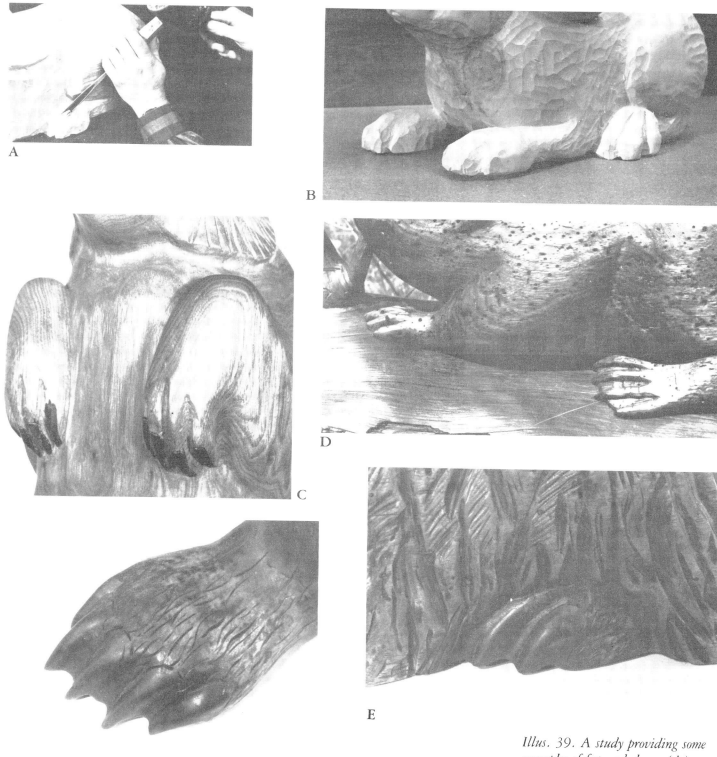

Illus. 39. A study providing some examples of feet and claws: (A) *snowshoe,* (B) *snowshoe,* (C) *prairie dog,* (D) *beaver,* (E) *badger (rear foot), and* (F) *badger (front foot).*

Carving Ears and Noses

Ears generally require some sort of hollowing operation. This can be accomplished using spoon-type gouges as shown in Illus. 40A. A die grinder is also useful for this type of shaping. Try to make the carvings so that the grain runs with the length of the ear. The jack rabbit ears, Illus. 40C, are a good example where maximum strength is necessary. Proper shape and texture of an ear is important. This effect can be achieved by slightly detailing with a V-parting tool, as shown in Illus.

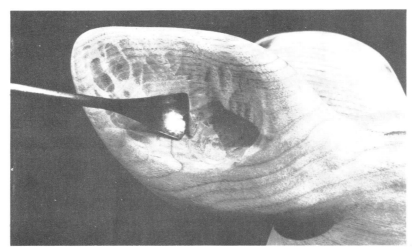

Illus. 40. A study, below and on facing page, shows examples of carved animal ears: (A) fawn, (B) fawn, (C) jack rabbit, (D) fox, (E) black bear, (F) fox, (G) snowshoe, (H) badger, (I) raccoon, (J) prairie dog.

A

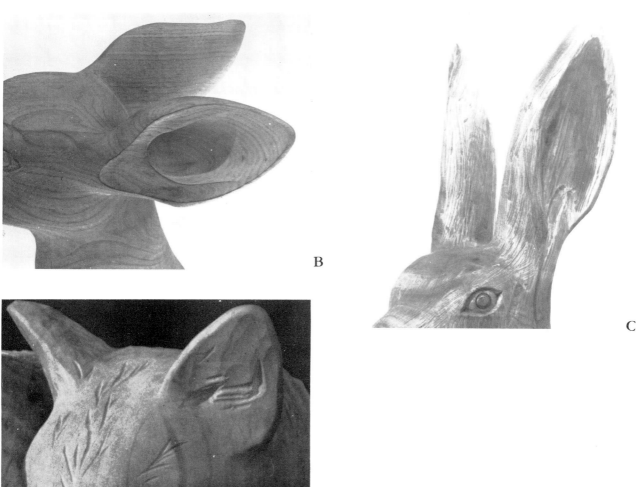

B

C

D

40D. Effective woodburning is shown in the badger and raccoon examples. See Illus. 40H and 40I. On some other animals it is desirable if the inside of the ear is simply smoothed in a concaved contour. See Illus. 40E, 40F, 40G, and 40J.

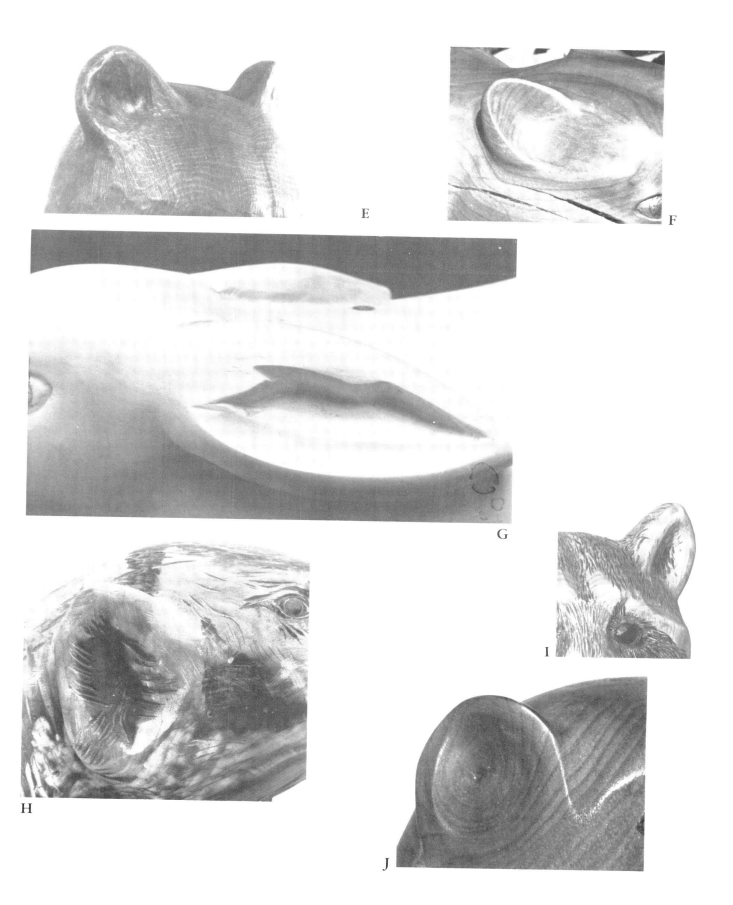

E

F

G

H

I

J

Illus. 41 compares a number of different animal noses. Some are easier and less involved to do than others. Work the carving to a particular shape as specified on the drawing. A good number of the animal carvings in this book have small nostril cavities that are carved in by hand. See Illus. 41A.

Illus. 41. A study below and on facing page provides some examples of animal noses: (A) badger, (B) badger, (C) badger, (D) fawn, (E) cougar, (F) cougar, (G) fox, (H) wolf, (I) wolf, (J) fox squirrel, (K) prairie dog, (L) mink, (M) beaver, (N) snowshoe, (O) black bear, (P) raccoon.

A

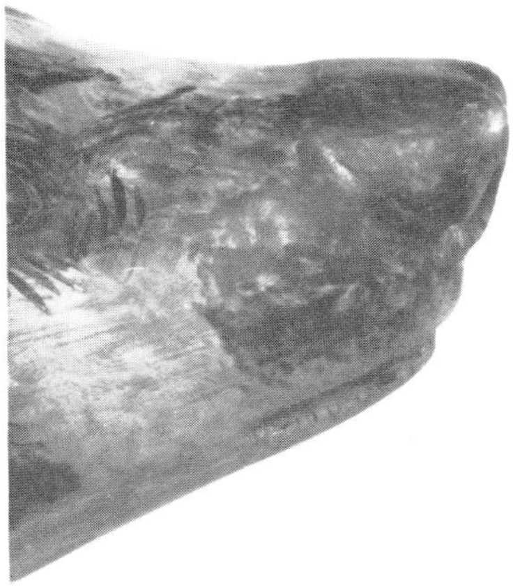

B

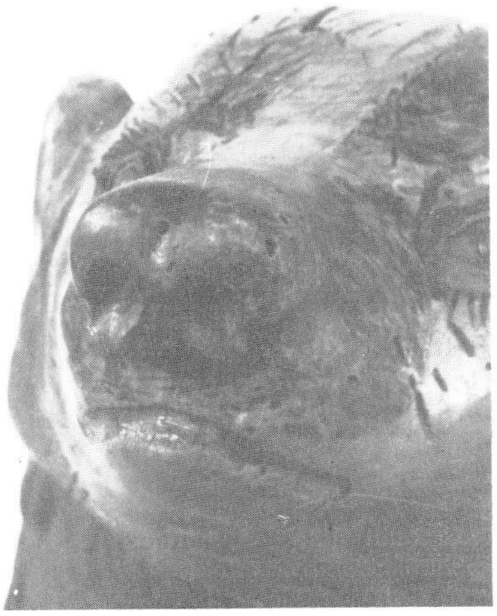

C

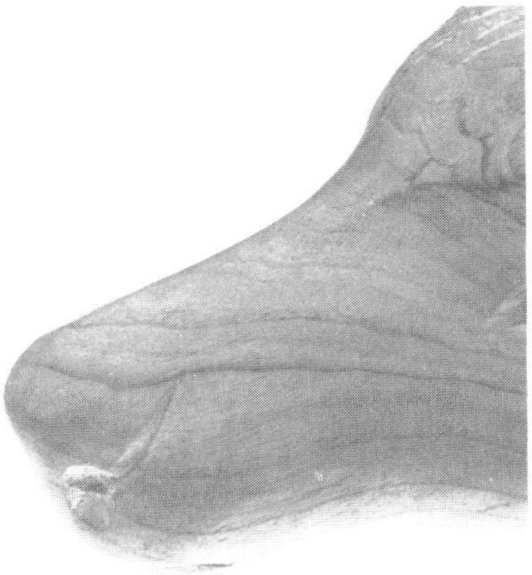

D

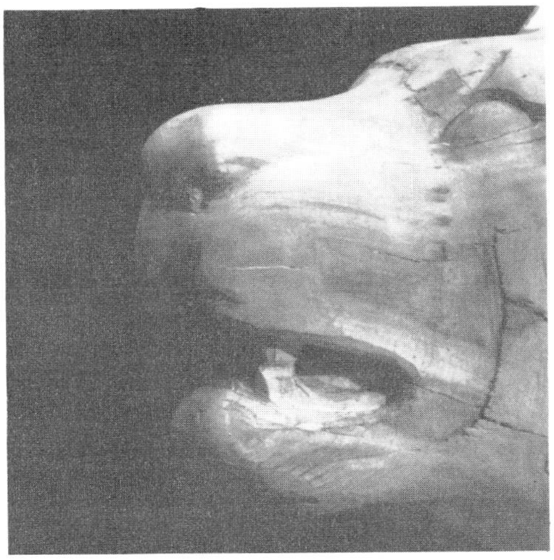

E

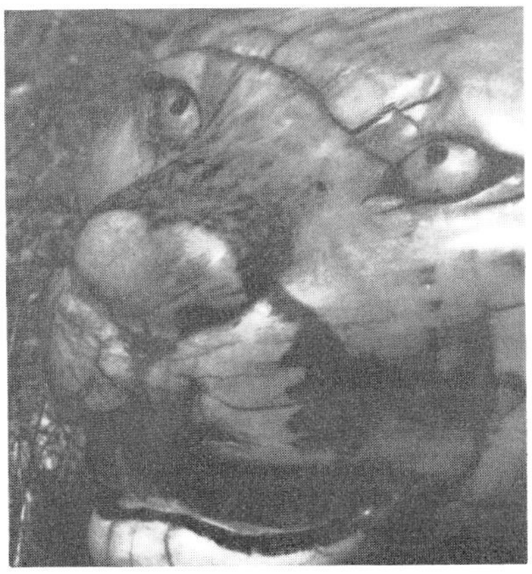

F

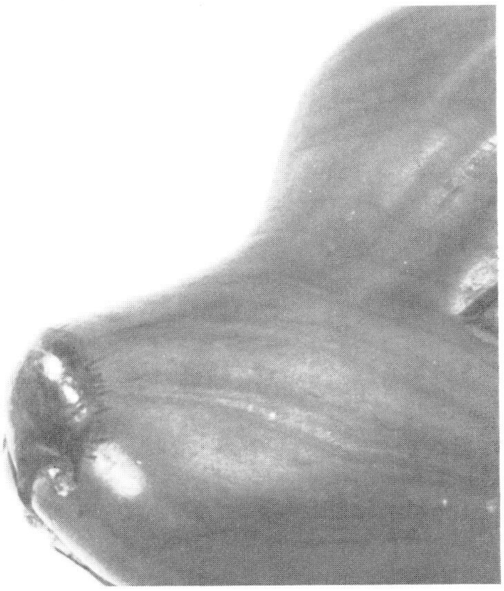

G

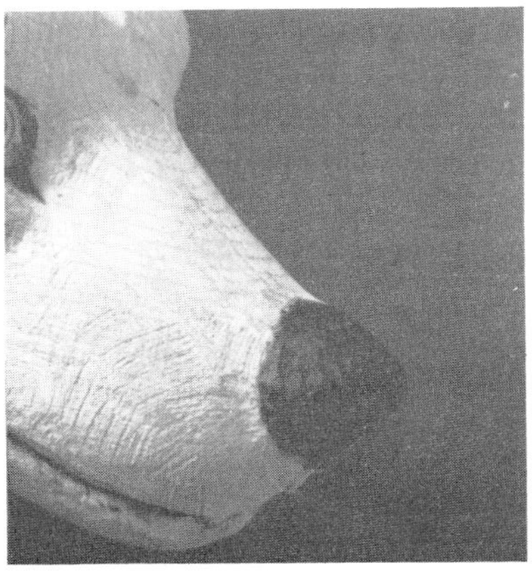

H

Once the shape is achieved many of the noses are made to appear black and glossy employing a woodburning technique. See Illus. 41B, 41C, 41G, 41H, and 41P for some typical examples. Sometimes the inside of the nostril is also darkened with the point of a woodburning tool. Other noses, such as that of the snowshoe are light in color.

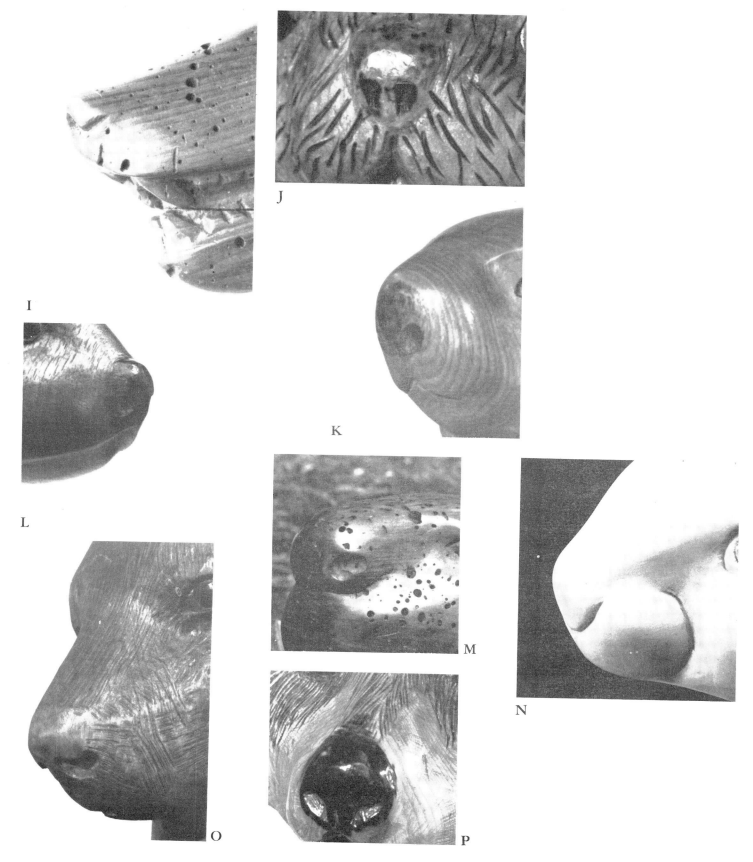

Carving Tails

The shape and position of the tail has a lot to do with the attitude and motion expressed by the animal. Animals use their tails as warning signals and for body balance. As you know, get out of the way of a skunk with its tail raised. If possible, the length of the tail on the carving should run with the grain of the wood. Most of the tails shown in Illus. 42 do, with the exception of parts of the skunk's tail. The cougar tail (Illus. 42A) was made from a branch coming out of a main trunk of the tree. The curl on the end of it does not reduce its strength at all. Refer to page 34 for more instructions concerning how the cougar is taken from the log.

Illus. 42. A study here and on the facing page provides some examples of carved animal tails: (A) cougar, (B) mink, (C) fox, (D) wolf, (E) skunk, (F) fawn, (G) beaver, (H) badger.

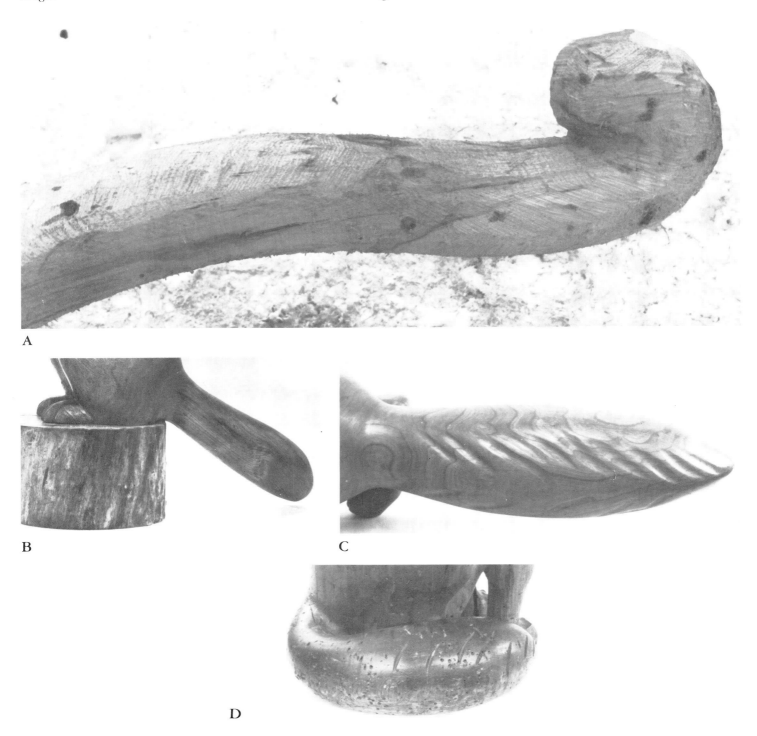

A

B

C

D

Notice how the curled tail of the wolf in Illus. 42D is designed to actually become part of the supporting base. Some tails are simply formed and sanded smooth (Illus. 42B), and others are textured in various ways. Texturing can be accomplished with a round file as on the fox's tail in Illus. 42C or done with a V-parting tool as on the badger (Illus. 42H). The woodburning tool is very effective in making the scaly tail of the beaver and it was also used to help simulate the shaggy hair of the badger's tail (Illus. 42H).

E

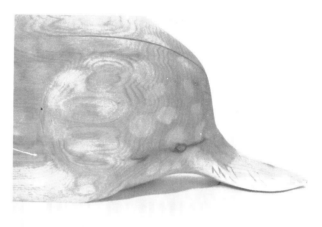

F

G

H

Wood and Finishing Techniques

Assuming you have some tools, you have to be motivated to take the first step. That is to go out and obtain some wood.

At first thought, the idea of securing pieces of wood in sizes suitable for carving large animals would seem to present some very serious problems. Not so. The authors are taking a very "commonsense approach" to this problematic subject. Just getting suitable wood is one "stumbling block" that often discourages and prevents wood carvers from creating anything with some size to it. The answer is to use common, locally available species of wood direct from the tree. Even consider those woods that are not normally used for carving or woodcrafting.

Sometimes you can find better and far more interesting wood than you can buy. It depends on how hard you look and search for it. In fact, sometimes it's free just for the sawing or hauling. The wood available locally may be quite a bit different from clear chunks of wood you might buy or laminate together to make flawless pieces.

If you're willing to accept some conditions that might otherwise be classified as defects, you will find an abundance of carving wood in any forest, woodlot, firewood pile, or even in your very own backyard. See Illus. 43 and 44.

Illus. 43 and 44. A box elder log being measured for a prospective carving.

Cougar, carved from box elder, with woodburned details and a natural oil finish.

Weasel, carved from a 2-inch cherry plank.

Red squirrel, carved from cherry.

B

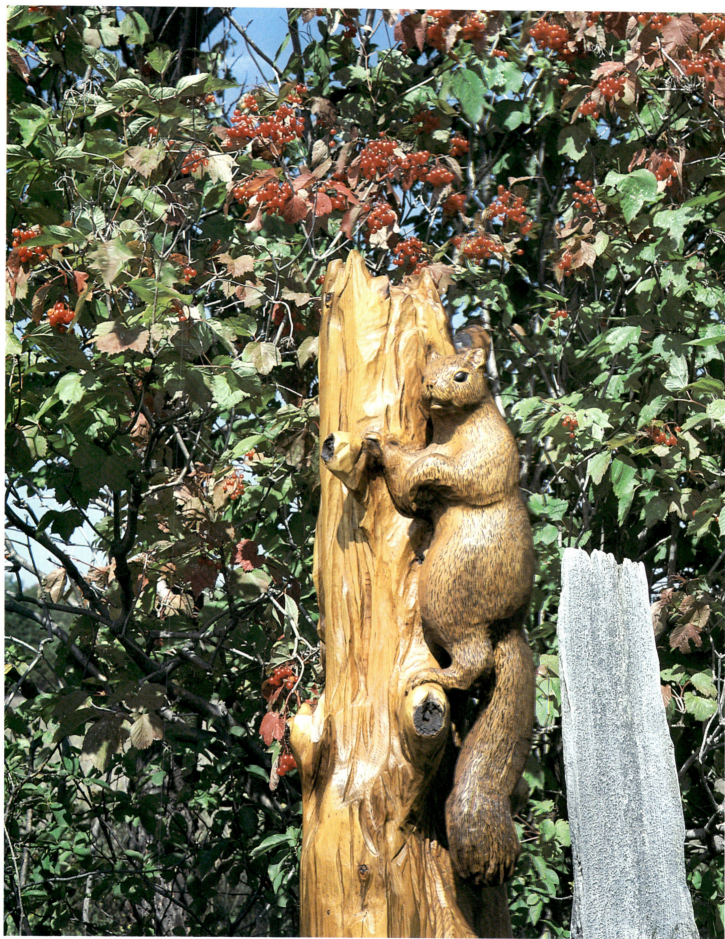

Fox squirrel, one-piece carving from white cedar.

Jack rabbit, carved of white cedar with natural finish.

D

Snowshoe rabbit, carved from box elder and bleached.

Cottontail in butternut.

Above, skunk in white cedar with bleached and charred finish.
Right, close-up of the skunk.

F

Prairie dog in natural butternut.

Howling wolf, carved from wormy butternut.

H

Mink, carved from natural butternut on a box elder base.

This large raccoon is a one-piece carving from white cedar.

Raccoon family, carved into an old cedar plank.

K

Beaver of solid wormy butternut on a pine slab base, with a closeup look below.

Fawn, carved from two pieces of solid butternut taken from the same log. Below is a closeup of the fawn's head. Note the woodburned details, bleaching around the ear and eye and the hairlines carved inside the ear.

Sleeping fox, carved from a box elder log section.

Above, stalking red fox,
carved in solid cherry.
Right, close-up of the stalking
red fox.

A one-piece carving of a black bear cub in white cedar with a dark oil finish and natural base. Note details in close-up.

P

Some of the kinds of woods used for the animals in this book include just a few of the many different kinds of wood available in northeast Wisconsin where I live. White cedar is a good wood for outdoor carvings. Butternut is one of this area's favorite woods. It is a dependable carving wood with a very pretty figure and color. It has good stability and also gets wormy. See the color section for examples.

Walnut is nice if you can find it, although it tends to crack easier in chunk form than many other woods. It has a beautiful dark brown color, and it finishes nicely. White ash has a darker heartwood and black ash is of a rich, brown coloring. Black cherry is recommended for the smaller carvings. You can expect it to crack if you use it for larger carvings. Refer to Illus. 45. Cherry is reddish brown in color.

A number of the larger animals were carved from box elder. This is a wood normally held in very low regard by most carvers and wood-workers. However, we think the results were very satisfactory and almost spectacular. Box elder is a creamy color with reddish streaks; a very striking combination. See Illus. 46. The list of suitable woods could go

Illus. 45. Dense, heavy hardwoods such as this cherry have greater tendencies to crack than do lower-density woods. Try to plan the carving so that if cracks develop, they will be to the bottom or the rear of the carving.

Illus. 46. A box elder log end. The central area often has unusual reds and orange coloring, along with a very light-colored outer wood. The gas-powered saw shown here is 16 inches which is suitable for most heavy cutting jobs.

on and on. The important thing is to look to the wood that is near you. Be observant for trees and stumps left when clearing wooded areas for housing developments, road construction, and trimming done in parks or the cleanup of fallen trees from storms, and so on.

Be sure to *analyze* and *study* the possibilities before you start sawing off any limbs. The cougar carving, for example, requires the limb still intact with the trunk. See Illus. 47. Try to visualize your carving within the wood as shown in the cougar example.

Illus. 47. Certain carvings will require some effort and creativity in finding the optimum material.

You may have to encounter conditions such as wormy wood, knots, dead limbs, decayed hollow sections, cracks, and splits. But don't panic; look at the many examples in this book to see how some of Mother Nature's effects can be used to create special points of interest or add unique qualities to the carving. Illus. 48 shows an animal rough-carved from a choice piece of wormy butternut. The wormy woods have become more popular in recent years. As a rule, wormy woods do not crack or split as readily as do other pieces of woods in the same species. Also, don't overlook wood marked by insect attack. See Illus. 49.

Illus. 48. Wormy wood, such as this rough-formed piece of butternut, makes some rare and special carvings.

Knots do not seriously detract from a carving, unless they are located in undesirable areas, such as near an eye or some place, which would make

Illus. 49. Insect tunnelling under the bark creates this special design effect naturally. This unusual effect can often be incorporated as a feature as shown on this integral base.

the carving of it more difficult or make the carving structurally weak. Knots, even decayed ones, on the back side or in the base of a carving do more to make the piece interesting than anything else.

When it comes right down to it, in order to have a good supply of carving wood, it is best to have a lot of it cut. Allow nature to dry it for as long as it takes, which may be a year or more for some woods. It's a good idea to cut dead or partially dry trees when possible to speed the drying process. With a plentiful supply of cut wood, you can pick and choose those pieces that are most suitable for the carving you have in mind. Thus, size needs and location of defects on the respective pieces can be considered for a specific carving. This is a far better approach than cutting only one piece and putting all of your hopes and work into it.

Roughing out a carving removes a large amount of the wood which reduces bulk, reduces stresses, and reduces the depths of existing cracks. If you take a green log and rough out a carving, it will dry faster and with shallower cracks than the whole log. Sometimes wood will not start cracking until it is almost dry. When you bring a piece indoors into the dry winter's artificial heat for its final drying stages, it may tend to crack. The best thing to do is just go ahead and carve. If cracks appear at this point or later in the curing or drying stages, you will just have to accept them. Be positive that luck will be on your side or if cracks appear they probably will not be all that disappointing. The impact of a carving and its overall shape is not destroyed with a crack. In fact, small cracks often enhance a carving (Illus. 50).

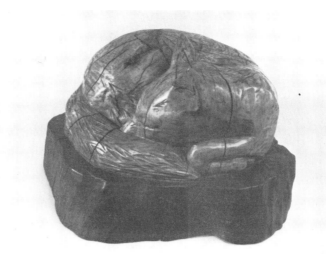

Illus. 50. This carving is a good example of where a lot of small cracks become a natural feature of the work.

It's best to observe your wood as you allow it to dry for a while (three months to a year) after cutting. It cracks develop, it's usually possible to work around them. Store your wood supply in the shade, in a protected area off the ground. Dead or fallen trees often have existing cracks that are either fully open or else the log will indicate with some checking where major cracks may develop later. It becomes a skill when selecting which part of a particular chunk of wood should be made into the front, side, and so on, of the animal. In case a crack should open up, it can be left as nature intended it to be or you can use a dark oil or stain to age the crack's inside surfaces. See Illus. 51.

Illus. 51. If cracks do appear in visible areas it's best to either leave them as is or to darken the inside surfaces of the crack with stain or wax, which often makes them more acceptable. We avoid attempting to fill cracks.

Usually, the beginning carver worries more about cracks than the experienced carver. In time, carvers become more used to accepting cracks. See Illus. 51 and 52. It is hard to predict where cracks and checks might develop. As a general rule, harder and denser woods tend to be more brittle and have greater tendencies to crack. Most often, slicing a big log into halves or quarters with a chain saw greatly reduces cracking possibilities. Some woods are hard and heavy, but they seem to be tough. A huge elm, for example, may not crack a whole lot because its cell or grain structure appears to be somewhat interwoven. Another general feeling is that knotty woods seem to crack less overall than do clear pieces of the same species.

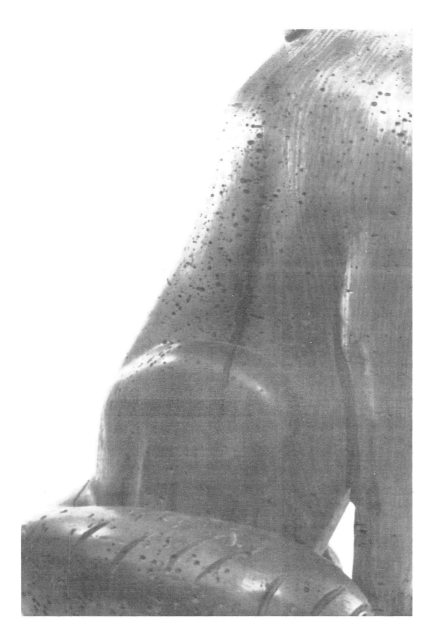

Illus. 52. A bark seam (crack) makes this dark streak.

Sometimes it's easier and more economical to use two separate pieces of wood (one for the head and one for the body) than to use one large log. The fawn carving is a good example of just such a carving. The head is glued and dowelled to the body in decoy fashion. See Illus. 53.

Illus. 53. A clear log, such as this one of butternut, offers less visual distraction for certain carving subjects. Here the head is cut from the same log as used for the body. The two parts are then joined with a dowel and glue.

Most of the animals in this book were finished naturally, as opposed to painting with heavily pigmented coating materials such as paint, enamels, or acrylics. Danish penetrating oils are available in a variety of transparent color tones. They are very easy to use. Soft woods, such as butternut and cedar, Illus. 54 and 55, absorb more finish than do denser woods like ash.

Illus. 54. Using a dark walnut transparent oil stain will change the appearance of the wood.

Illus. 55. Oil finishes deepen and enhance the figure and pattern of the wood. They also harden the surface and all finishes should be followed with wax for added protection.

Sometimes you will want white or lighter underparts of the animal to be emphasized, with the rest of the carving to remain natural. In such areas, wood bleach can be used effectively. Bleach was used on several carvings in this book. Some specific features of the fawn were also bleached. See Illus. 56.

Waxing is the final step. The carvings in this book were waxed with either a light- or a dark-colored liquid wax or a mixture of light and dark wax. A considerable amount of time was devoted to polish each carving to enhance to maximum the natural beauty of the wood.

Illus. 56. Employing the bleaching technique gives a different characteristic to the wood.

Sanding a carving can involve a lot of time. Not all carvings should be or need to be sanded or sanded that well. If you desire a smooth or glassy surface, it's hard to be too thorough. The overall quality of the finish and the final appearance of carvings obviously hinges on the quality and effort put into sanding.

Finishing involves all of those operations that follow final sanding. This includes woodburning details and signing your name on the bottom.

2

ANIMALS
AND PATTERNS

Weasel

Weasels in their white winter coats are known as ermine. This fur-bearing family includes martens, badgers, skunks, and otters. They are carnivorous with a strong, unpleasant odor and are quick-moving slim animals.

The long-tailed weasel is the best known. It has a white belly and dark-brown back with a black tip on its tail. The female is about 13 inches long and the male 16 inches. The short-tailed weasel is smaller, averaging 9–11 inches.

The least weasel is also one of the smallest carnivorous animals being 6–8 inches long.

Illus. 57. This solid cherry weasel is a one-piece carving.

Illus. 58. Weasel side view. Note the front left foot is slightly forward.

Illus. 59. Weasel side view.

Illus. 60. Weasel top view.

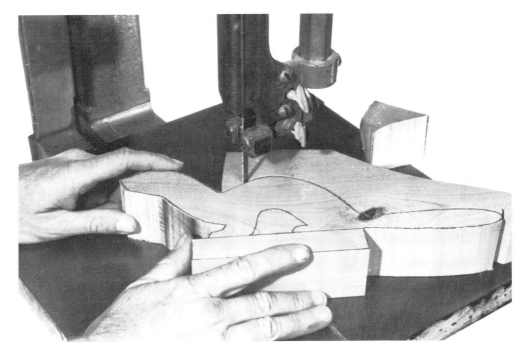

Illus. 61. Band-sawing the weasel from a block of 2-inch cherry.

Illus. 62. Boring and drilling, as shown here, can be an effective stock-removal technique.

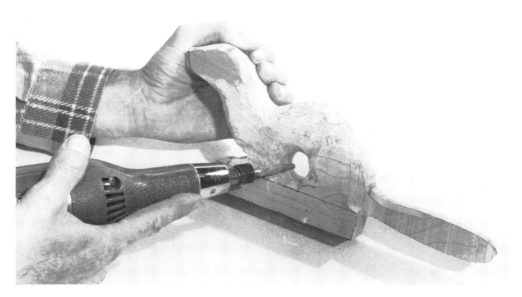

Illus. 63. Using a die grinder and bit to rough out the shape.

Illus. 64. Close-up of the weasel head.

Illus. 65. Frontal close-up of the weasel head.

Illus. 66. Pattern for long-tailed weasel. 1" = 1"

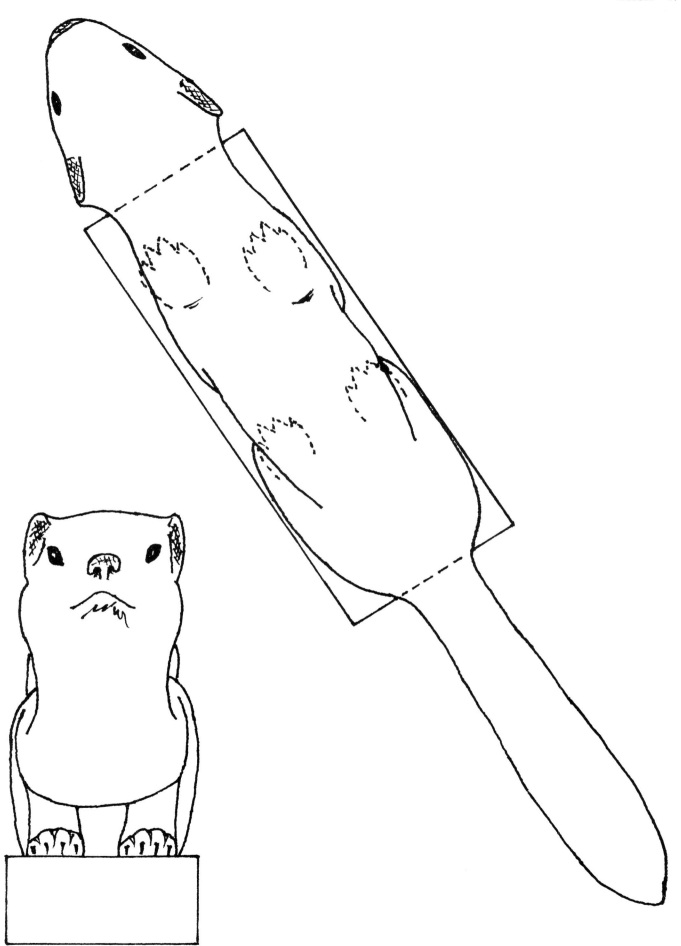

Illus. 66 (cont.). 1″ = 1″

Red Squirrel

Red squirrels are of a large family of rodents. They have chisel-like front teeth, useful for gnawing. They are the most active and noisiest of all the squirrels. They often cut down pine cones and hide them in hollow tree stumps or under stones and roots.

Few red squirrels are over a foot long, including the tail. They weigh 5–11 ounces. The fur is reddish on the backs and some have a line of dark fur separating the red from the white fur on the underparts.

Twice a year the female gives birth to 2–6 young, after a gestation period of 36–45 days. Newborn squirrels have no fur and their eyes are closed. Their life-span is 2–6 years in the wild and up to 15 years in captivity.

Illus. 67. Red squirrel is carved of cherry and glued to separate base.

Illus. 68. Red squirrel—top view.

Illus. 69. Red squirrel—side view.

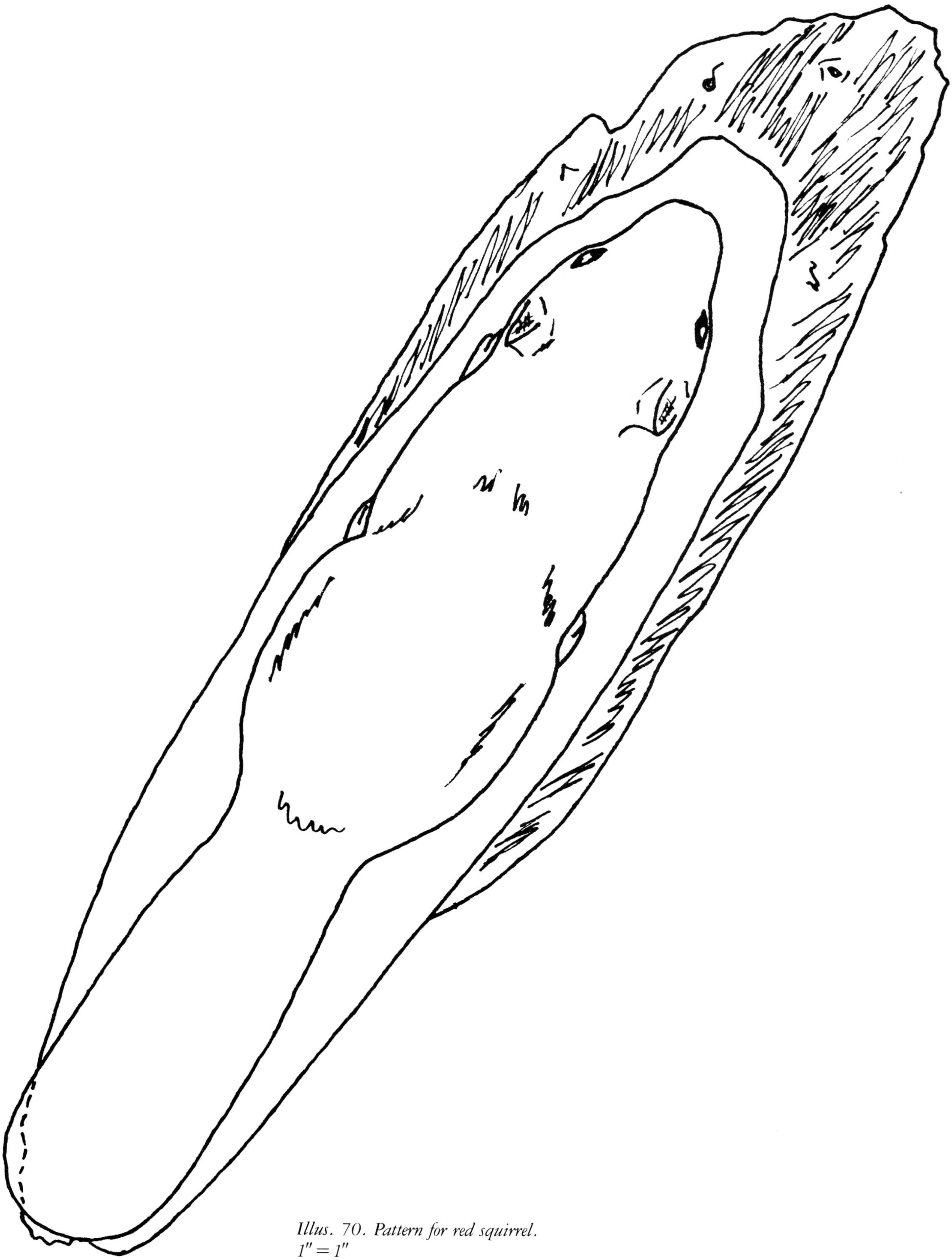

Illus. 70. Pattern for red squirrel.
1" = 1"

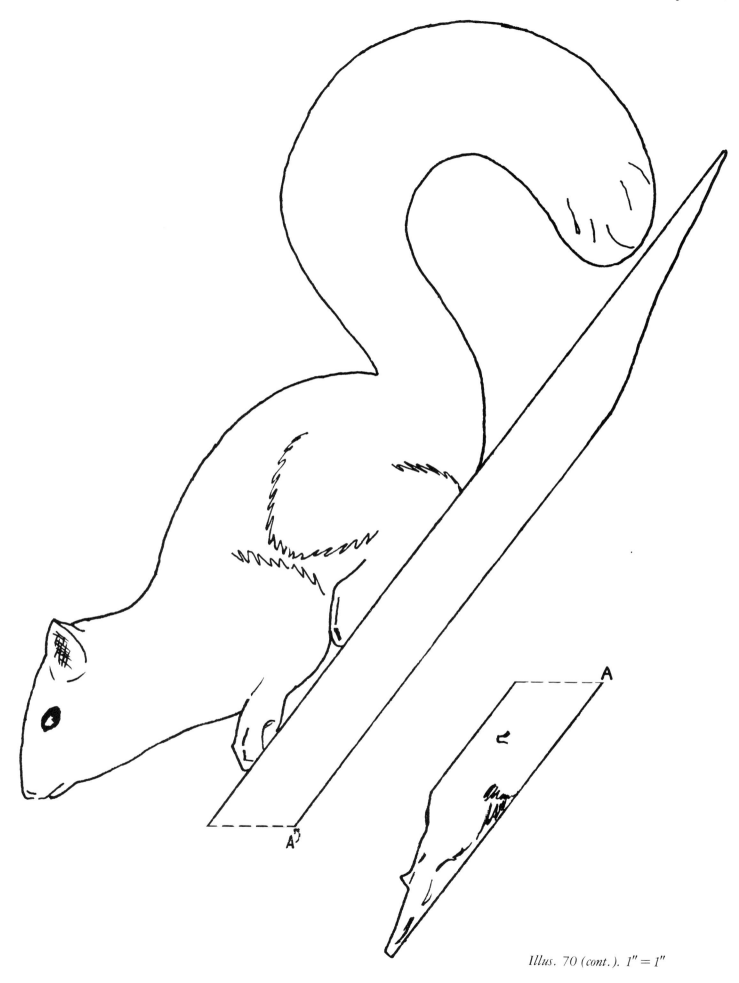

Illus. 70 (cont.). 1″ = 1″

Fox Squirrel

The largest of tree squirrels, the fox squirrel is either black, a rusty color, or grey. It weighs up to 3 pounds and can be 2 feet in length, including up to 10 inches in tail length. It spends a lot of time on the ground and is found mostly in the eastern half of the United States. They have constantly growing incisors which wear down as they eat hard foods. Fox squirrels eat acorns, other nuts and seeds and buds.

Its senses are keen; especially its sense of smell.

They average 3 to a litter and are born without hair and with eyes closed. They are most active during the day. Snakes are an enemy to young squirrels; hawks are an enemy to adults.

Illus. 71. Fox squirrel.

Illus. 72. Side view of fox squirrel.

Figure 73. Front view of fox squirrel with base. This is a one-piece carving made from a white cedar log.

Figure 74. Fox squirrel—rear view.

Figure 75. Another view of the fox squirrel's carved base. (Squirrel is hidden on other side.)

Figure 76. Side view of rough-formed squirrel and base.

Illus. 77. Front view in the rough. This particular log came from an old log barn.

Figure 78. Rear view of roughed-out carving.

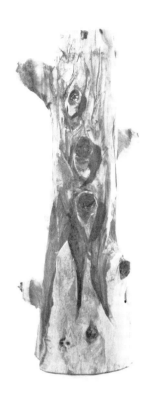

Illus. 79. Opposite side of fox squirrel carving. Chain saw was used to cut knots into high relief, as shown here.

Illus. 80. Die grinder has been used to remove chain-sawn roughness.

Figure 81. A close-up, showing final shaping with the die grinder.

Illus. 82. Shaping the tail.

Illus. 83. Fox squirrel upper-body details.

Illus. 84. Head detail of the fox squirrel.

Illus. 85. Another close-up look at the fox squirrel head.

Illus. 86. A close look at the completed squirrel lower body.

Illus. 87. Side, front and rear view patterns of the fox squirrel carving. ¼" = 1"

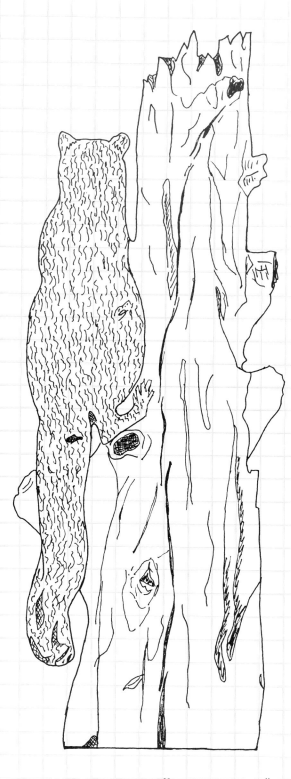

Illus. 87 (cont.). ¼″ = 1″

Varying Hare or Snowshoe

In winter, the hare's brown coat of fur is replaced by white fur for camouflage. The large furry hind feet or "snowshoes," enable it to move about in deep, soft snow. Adults are about 15–20 inches long and weigh about 3 or 4 pounds. Males are somewhat larger than females.

It has an acute sense of hearing, scent, and eyesight.

Its range includes Alaska, Canada, and the northern parts of the United States.

Two or three litters per year are common, sometimes more. The young hares are born with fur and open eyes. They are a food source for animals and some birds of prey.

The snowshoe feeds upon bark, twigs, grasses, and other forms of vegetation. It is a fast animal and can run up to 30 miles per hour and jump up to 10 feet or more.

Illus. 88. Snowshoe is carved from any light-colored wood.

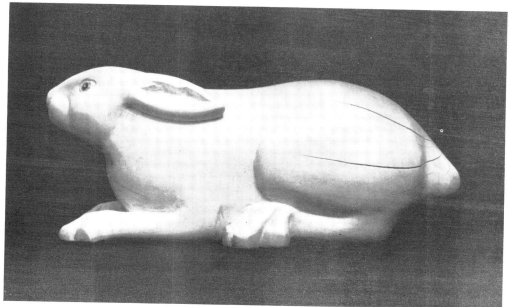

Illus. 89. Side view.

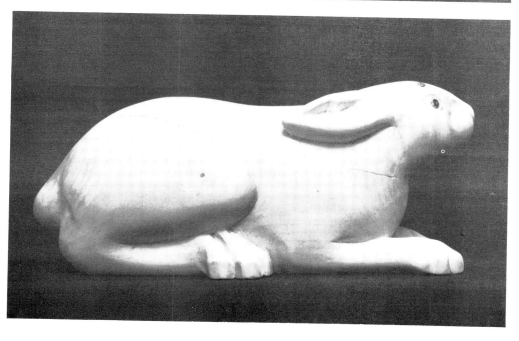

Illus. 90. Side view.

Illus. 91. Front view.

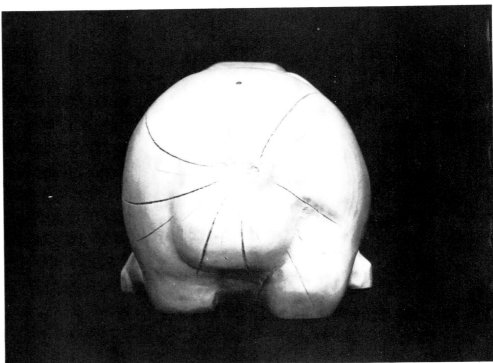

Illus. 92. Rear view. Note: *Radial checking from pith.*

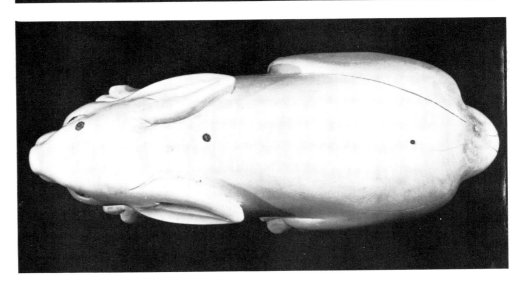

Illus. 93. Top view.

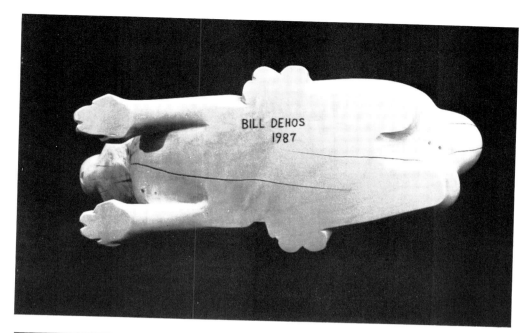

Illus. 94. Bottom view.

Illus. 95. Roughing-out the snowshoe from a box elder log.

Illus. 96. Side view of roughed-out snowshoe.

Illus. 97. Side view of roughed-out snowshoe.

Illus. 98. The front view in the rough.

Illus. 99. Rear view of roughed-out snowshoe.

Illus. 100. Top view of chain-sawn rough shape.

Illus. 101. The bottom view of rough chain-sawn shape.

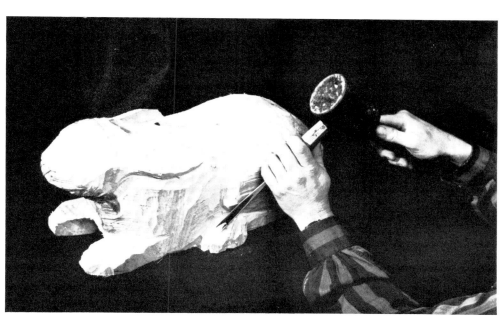

Illus. 102. Beginning to shape the foot; V-parting tool separates the toes.

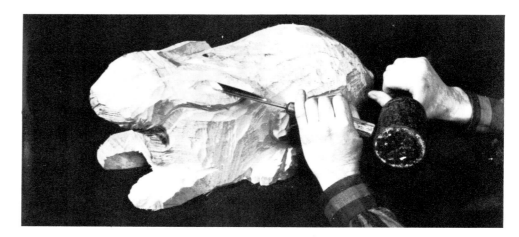

Illus. 103. Hollowing out the ear.

Illus. 104. Preliminary shaping of the eye begins with the V-parting tool, as shown.

Illus. 105. Initial chisel and gouge cuts start to show details emerging from the chain-sawn form.

Illus. 106. Sanding to remove chisel marks.

Illus. 107. Bleached box elder makes the perfect white look for the snow-shoe.

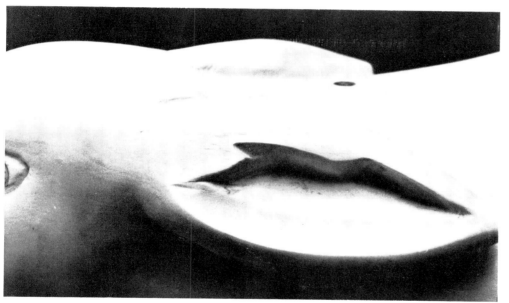

Illus. 108. Close-up of snowshoe's ear detail.

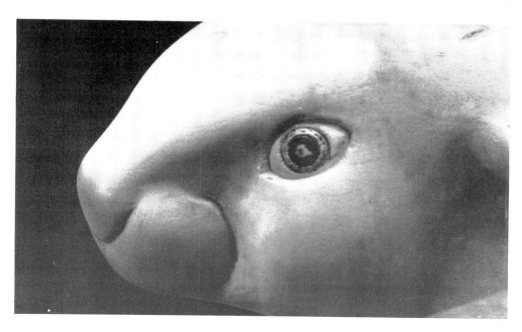

Illus. 109. Close-up of snowshoe eye and nose details.

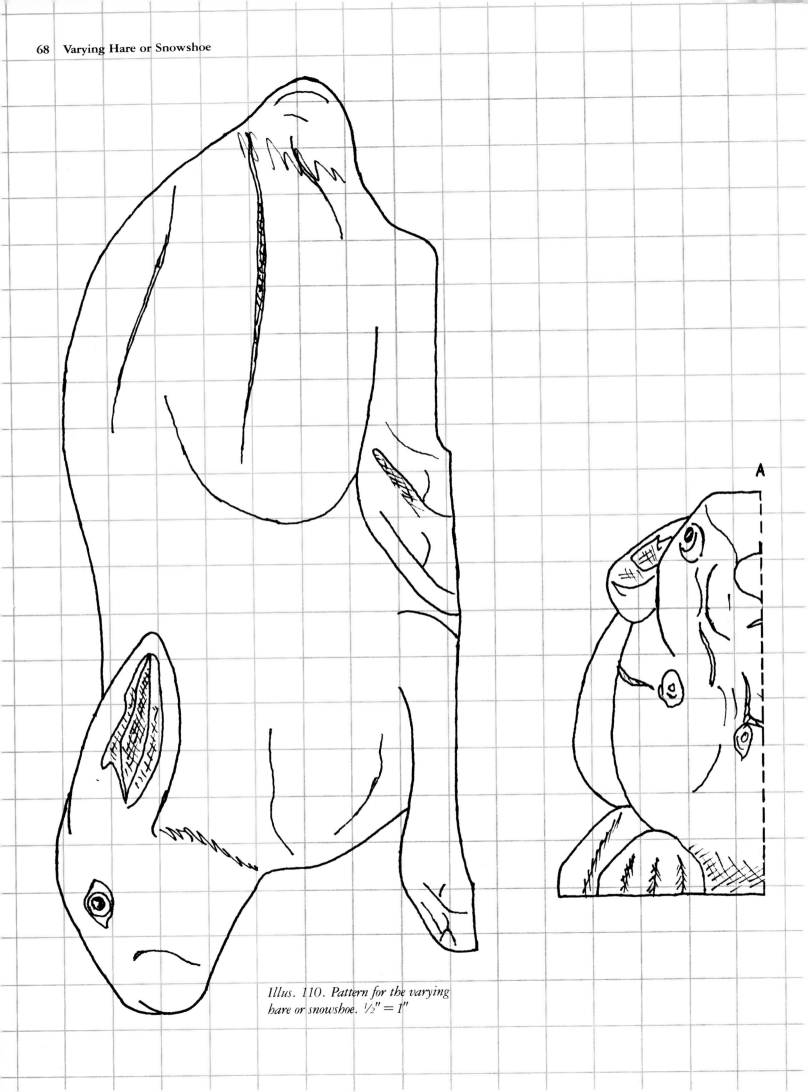

Illus. 110. Pattern for the varying hare or snowshoe. ½" = 1"

A

Illus. 110 (cont.). ½" = 1"

Cottontail Rabbit

Cottontails are small, about 14–18 inches in length. They have a basic body color of brown with white underparts and tails. Females are slightly larger than males.

The eastern cottontail is found east of the Rocky Mountains, and inhabits any area with adequate cover and food supply. Rabbits eat vegetation including shrub and tree bark.

They can run up to 20 miles an hour and have keen senses.

High numbers are taken by animals and birds of prey, but the population is maintained by the cottontail's ability to have 3–4 litters per year. The young rabbits are born almost furless and with closed eyes.

Illus. 111. Cottontail rabbit in butternut.

Illus. 112. Cottontail side view.

Illus. 113. Front view of the cottontail rabbit.

Illus. 114. Side view. Note the animal's tail is lightened with wood bleach.

Illus. 115. Cottontail rear view.

Illus. 116. Here are two other small cottontails: The one on the left is of butternut, and the one on the right is of cedar.

Illus. 117. Pattern for the cottontail rabbit. (Continued on next page.)
³⁄₄″ = 1″

Illus. 117 (cont.). ¾" = 1"

Illus. 117 (cont.). ¾" = 1"

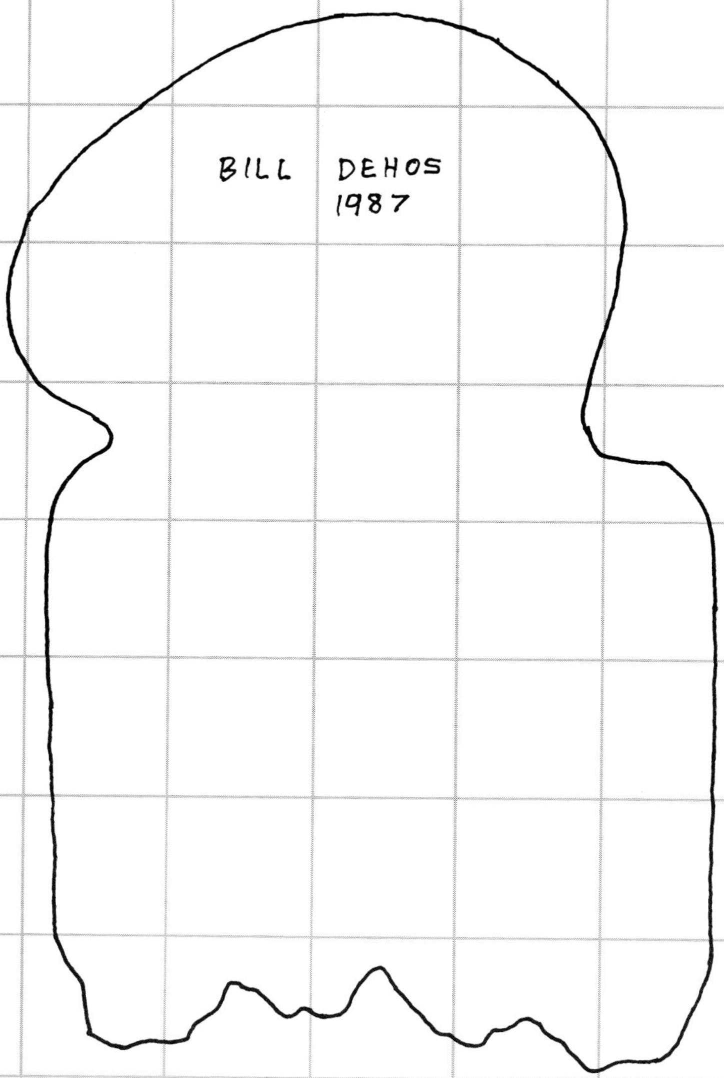

BILL DEHOS
1987

Illus. 118. Pattern, showing bottom
view of cottontail. ¾" = 1"

Jack Rabbit

The jack rabbit is a hare, not a rabbit, because its young are born with open eyes and fur.

The white-tailed jack rabbits are about 22–26 inches long, including the tail, and average about 8 pounds. Black-tailed jack rabbits are a little smaller and lighter.

Jack rabbits have very long ears and can hear the slightest sound. They live in open areas and do a lot of feeding at night.

Illus. 119. Jack rabbit, carved from an old cedar barn log.

Illus. 120 and 121. Front and rear views.

Illus. 122. Side view.

Illus. 123. Side view.

Illus. 124. Undercutting the front paws of the jack rabbit.

Illus. 125. Hollowing the base minimizes possible checking and cracking.

Illus. 126. Front view of the jack rabbit in the rough.

Illus. 127. Rear view. Try to orient carvings so that existing cracks will be to the rear.

Illus. 128. A side view in the rough.

Illus. 129. The roughed-out jack rabbit, as cut with the chain saw. Note the character features of the old wood. The color is deepened and varied along with the wormholes and checks typical of well-aged wood.

Illus. 130. The other side view, showing the rough shape.

Illus. 131. Close-up of the feet and base, as chain sawn.

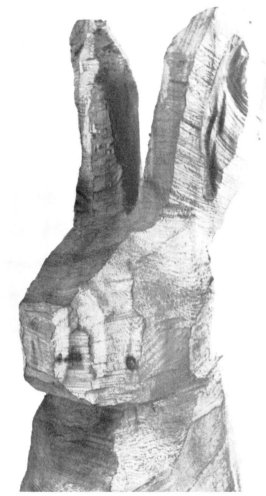

Illus. 132. A look at the head immediately following the chain-saw roughing operation.

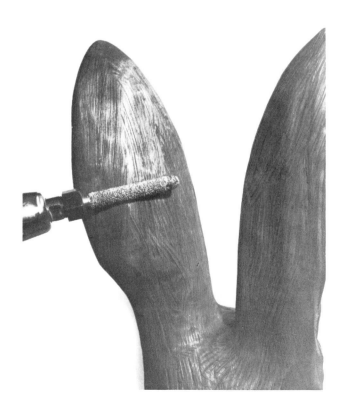

Illus. 133. Forming the convex contour of the jack rabbit's ears.

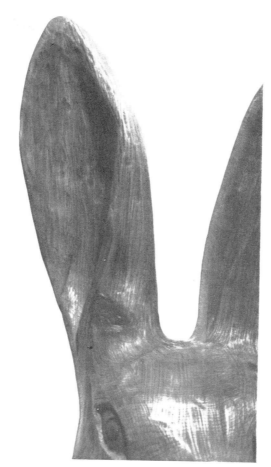

Illus. 134. Close-up shows the concave hollowing of the ear.

Illus. 136. Base of the jack rabbit carving shows the interesting design made by insects tunnelling under the bark.

Illus. 135. Head details of the jack rabbit.

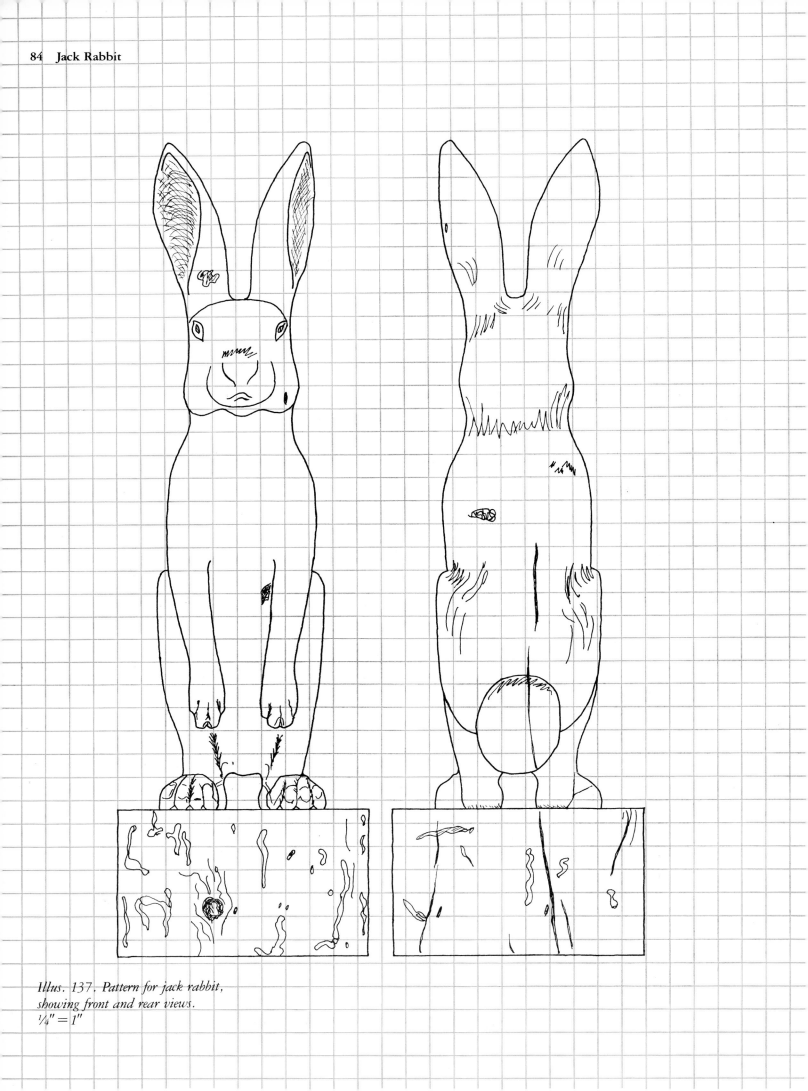

*Illus. 137. Pattern for jack rabbit,
showing front and rear views.*
¼" = 1"

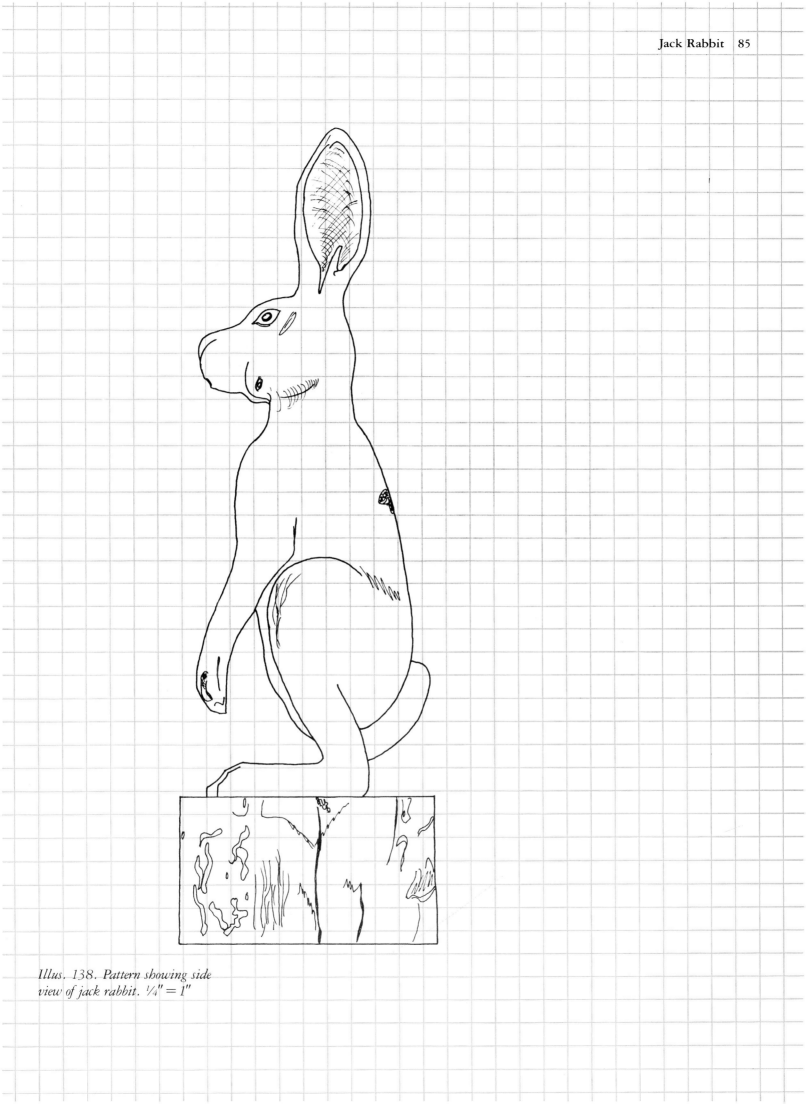

Illus. 138. Pattern showing side view of jack rabbit. ¼″ = 1″

Skunk

The skunk is the size of a large house cat and has distinctive black and white markings. There are two glands near the tail that squirt a vile-smelling fluid, with a range of up to 10 feet, when it is defending itself from its enemies. Skunks are active at night and sleep during the day. In the winter, several skunks may use the same den to sleep in, but they don't truly hibernate.

Skunks are helpful to the farmers for they eat rats, mice, and other small animals that damage crops. But, they also raid hen roosts to eat eggs.

Since their long, thick and shiny fur is attractive and wears well, its pelt is highly prized. But not as highly as that of the mink.

Illus. 139. Skunk carving.

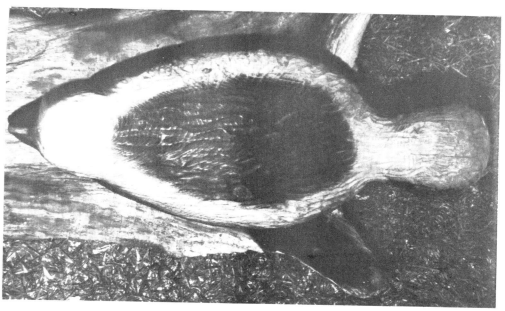

Illus. 140. A top view of the skunk.

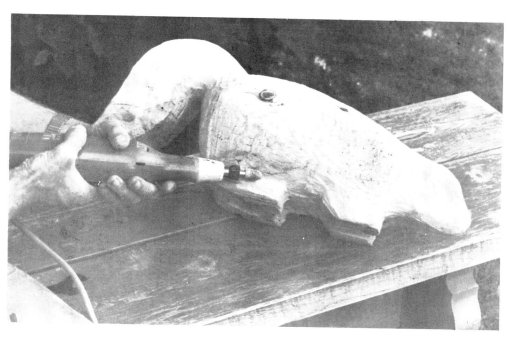

Illus. 141. Contouring the body to the legs.

Illus. 142. Texturing the skunk's fluffy tail.

Illus. 143. Working on the nose with the die grinder.

Illus. 144. Shaping the head.

Illus. 145. Final rough-shaping completed.

Illus. 146. Side view of the skunk, ready for smoothing.

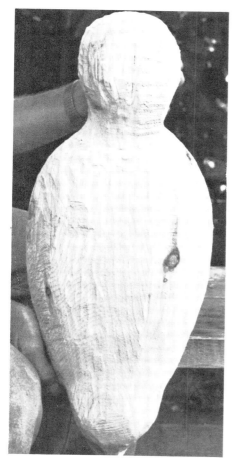

Illus. 148. Skunk, carved of cedar, has charred and bleached striping. The base is a piece of stump burned in a forest fire.

Illus. 147. Looking at the top of the skunk carving.

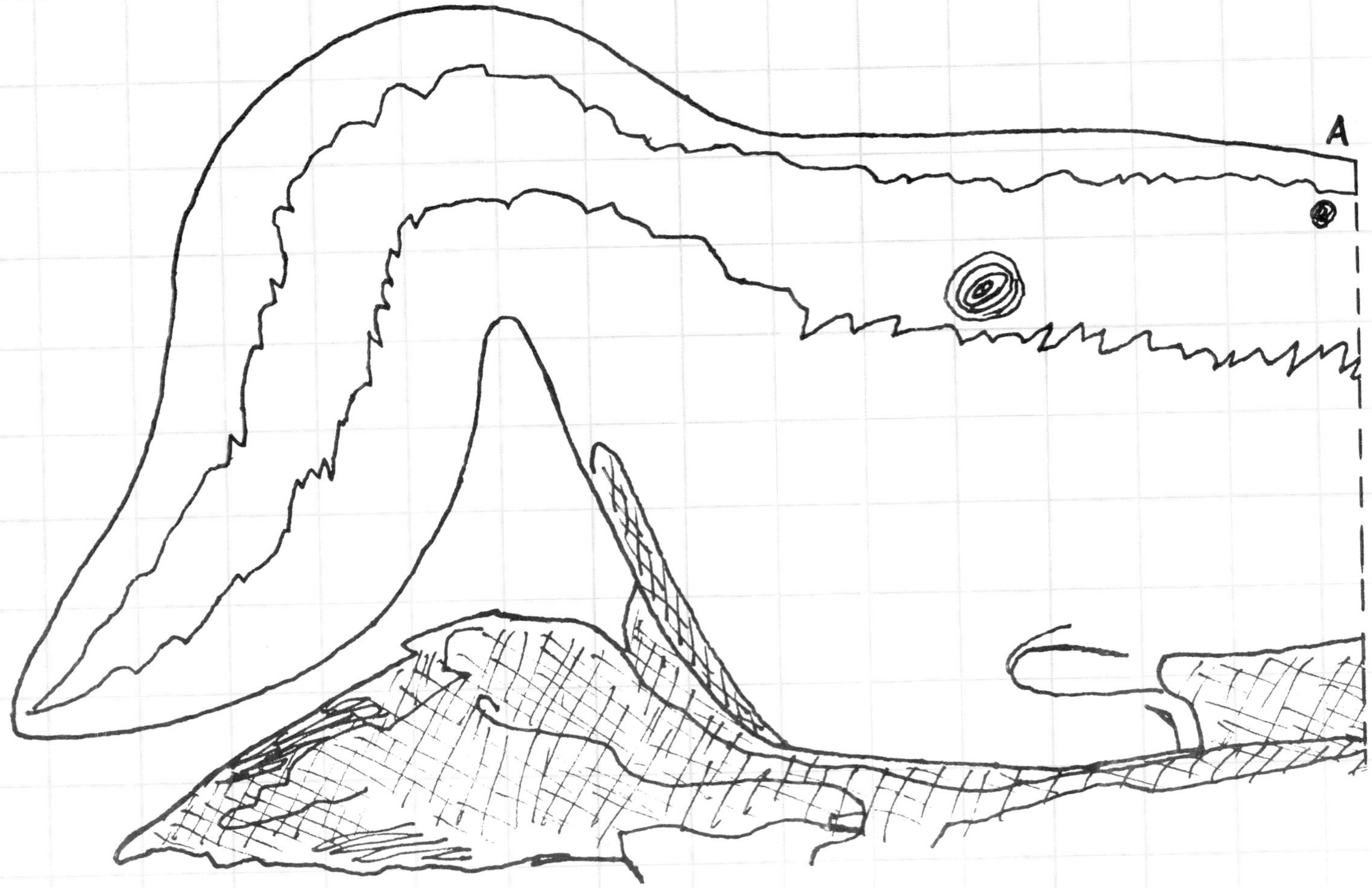

*Illus. 149. Patterns showing various
views of the skunk carving. Top view
shows an optional base.* ½″ = 1″

Illus. 149 (cont.). ½″ = 1″

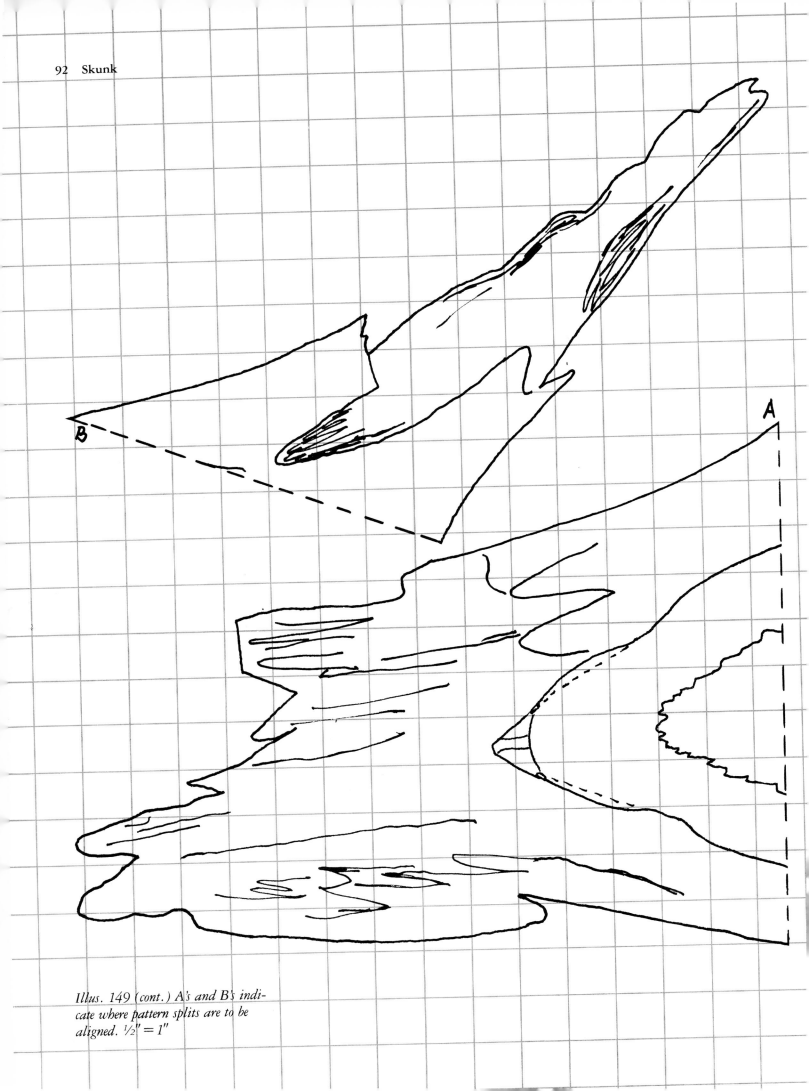

Illus. 149 (cont.) A's and B's indi-
cate where pattern splits are to be
aligned. ½" = 1"

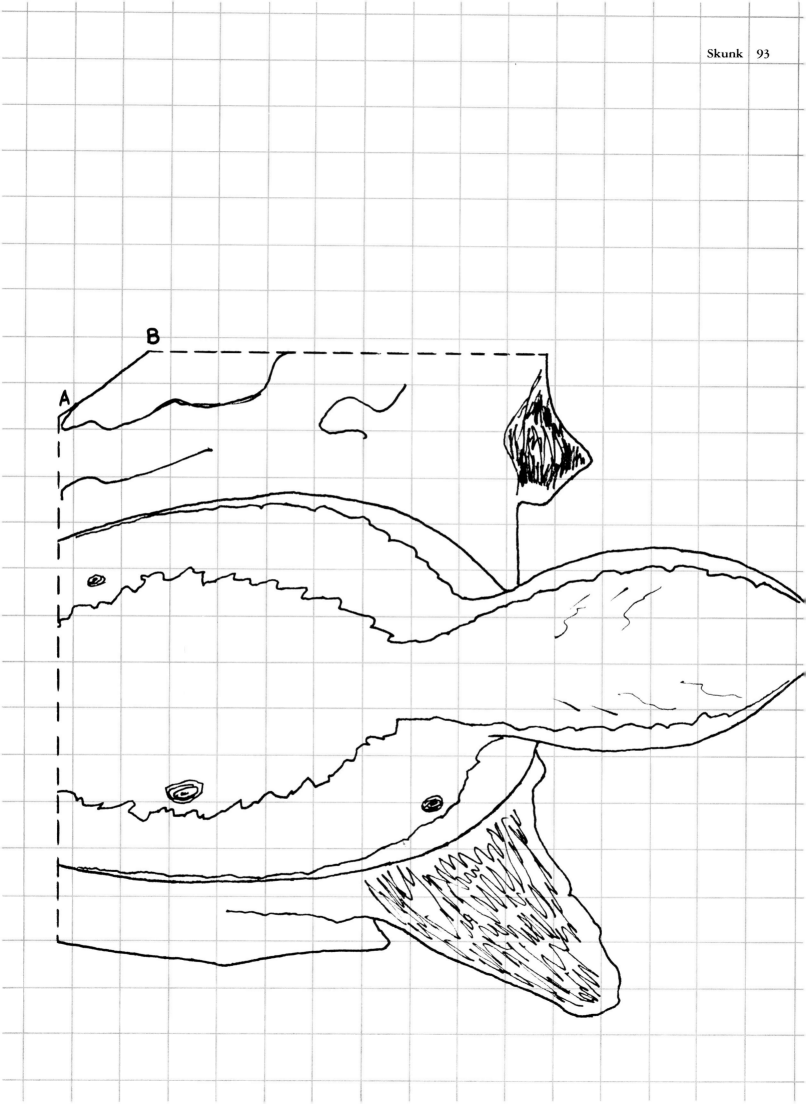

Illus. 149 (cont.). ½" = 1"

Prairie Dog

The prairie dog has a coarse, greyish-brown fur and is about a foot long. It got its name from the shrill doglike bark that it makes to warn others that danger is near. It lives in communities with other prairie dogs, in burrows 12 feet deep with many chambers or rooms for sleeping and storage. They mound the dirt up around the entrance to prevent water from flooding out their homes.

The prairie dog spends the winter in his home and comes out on sunny days. The enemies of the prairie dog are rattlesnakes, coyotes, and man. Man is his enemy, because the burrows are hazardous to horses and cattle, which might break a leg by stepping into one of the holes.

Illus. 150. Prairie dog of solid butternut.

Illus. 151. Front view.

Illus. 152. Prairie dog side view. Tail is inserted separately, dowel fashion, into the body. See Illus. 158.

Illus. 153. Side view of prairie dog. Note the beautiful grain (figure) of the butternut used for this carving.

Illus. 154. Head close-up. Note the realistic eye and nose details achieved by employing a combination of carving and woodburning techniques.

Illus. 155. Another head close-up shows simple concave shapes for the ear and eye sockets.

Illus. 156. Front legs and body details.

Illus. 157. Close-up of rear leg details. Note the lifelike, hard, glossy look of the claws that's accomplished with a burning tool.

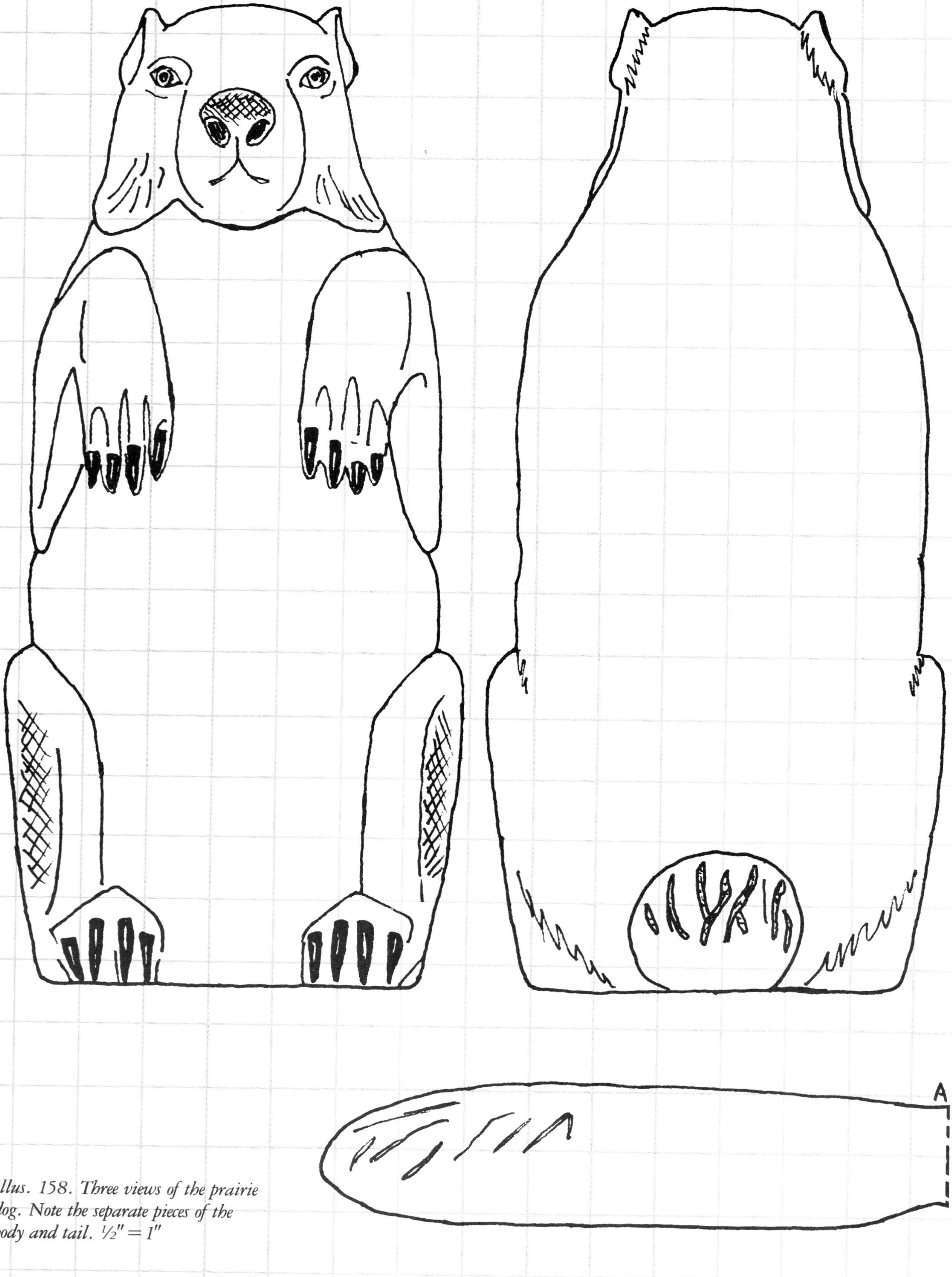

Illus. 158. Three views of the prairie dog. Note the separate pieces of the body and tail. ½" = 1"

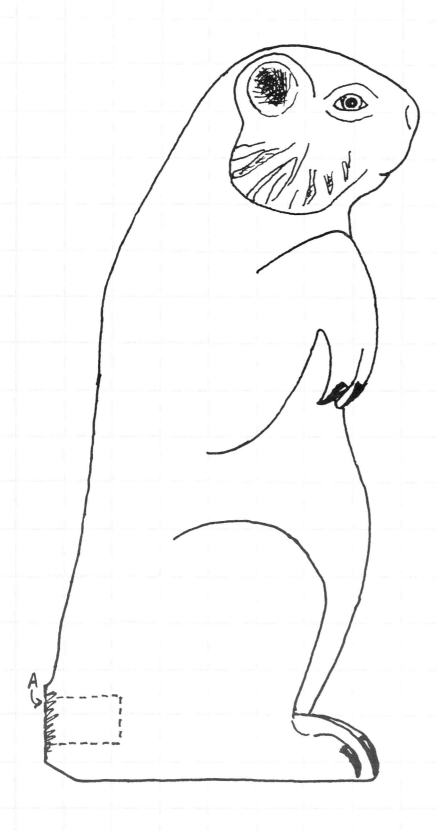

A

Illus. 158 (cont.). ½″ = 1″

Mink

ale minks are between 14 to 25 inches long with bushy tails that extend another 8–9 inches. They stand 4–5 inches at the shoulders and sometimes weigh 2 pounds. The female is smaller and weighs half as much as the male. The color ranges from light brown or tan to a dark chocolate color with white patches on the chin and spots of white on the throat and chest in the wild, and from white and pale silver to darkest brown in captivity. Like its cousin the skunk, it has a strong odor but can't spray its scent at a distance.

The mink has a litter of 4 to 10 kits in the spring. The family stays together until early fall when the young scatter to find hunting ranges of their own.

Illus. 159. Mink is carved of butter-nut with an oil finish.

Illus. 160. A front view.

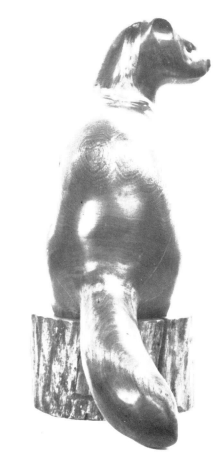

Illus. 161. Rear view.

Illus. 162. Side view.

Illus. 163. Side view.

Illus. 164. Here's how to cut the mink from the log.

Illus. 165. Rough chain-sawn top and bottom views.

Illus. 166. Here's how it looks immediately following the chain-sawing.

Illus. 167. A separate base of box elder. Lag bolts are countersunk appropriately.

Illus. 168. A gouge removes chain-saw roughness and refines the shape.

Illus. 169. Close-up of the mink head. Note how similar this ear is to that of the prairie dog shown on page 27.

Illus. 170. Front head close-up of the mink.

Illus. 171. Dark transparent oil is used for first coat to achieve the desired color. Apply additional coats of natural oil for greater depth, lustre, and protection.

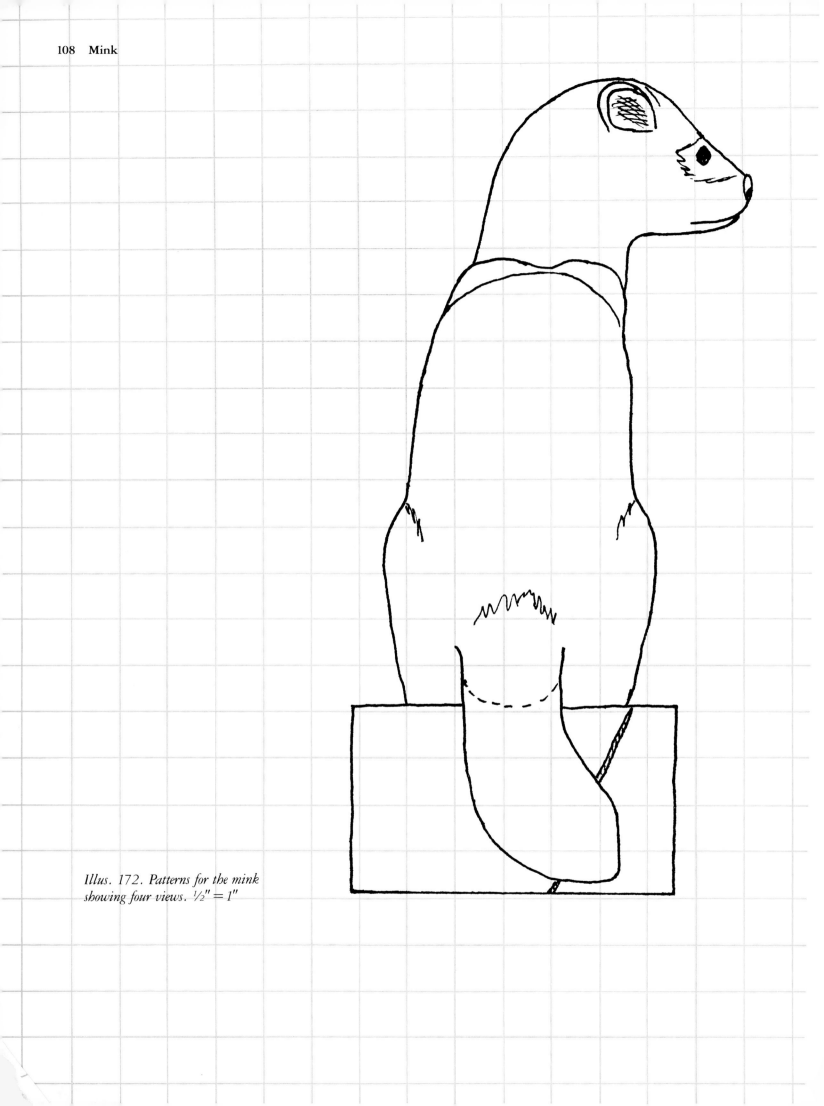

Illus. 172. Patterns for the mink showing four views. ½" = 1"

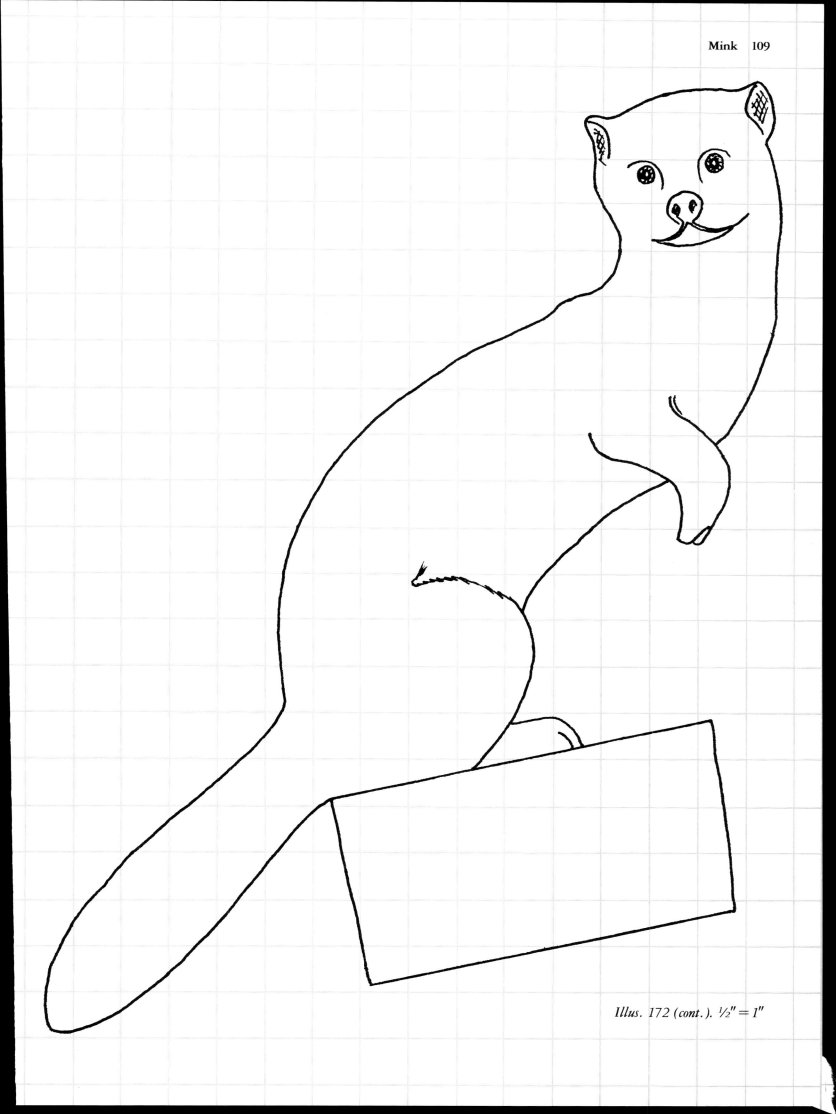

Illus. 172 (cont.). ½" = 1"

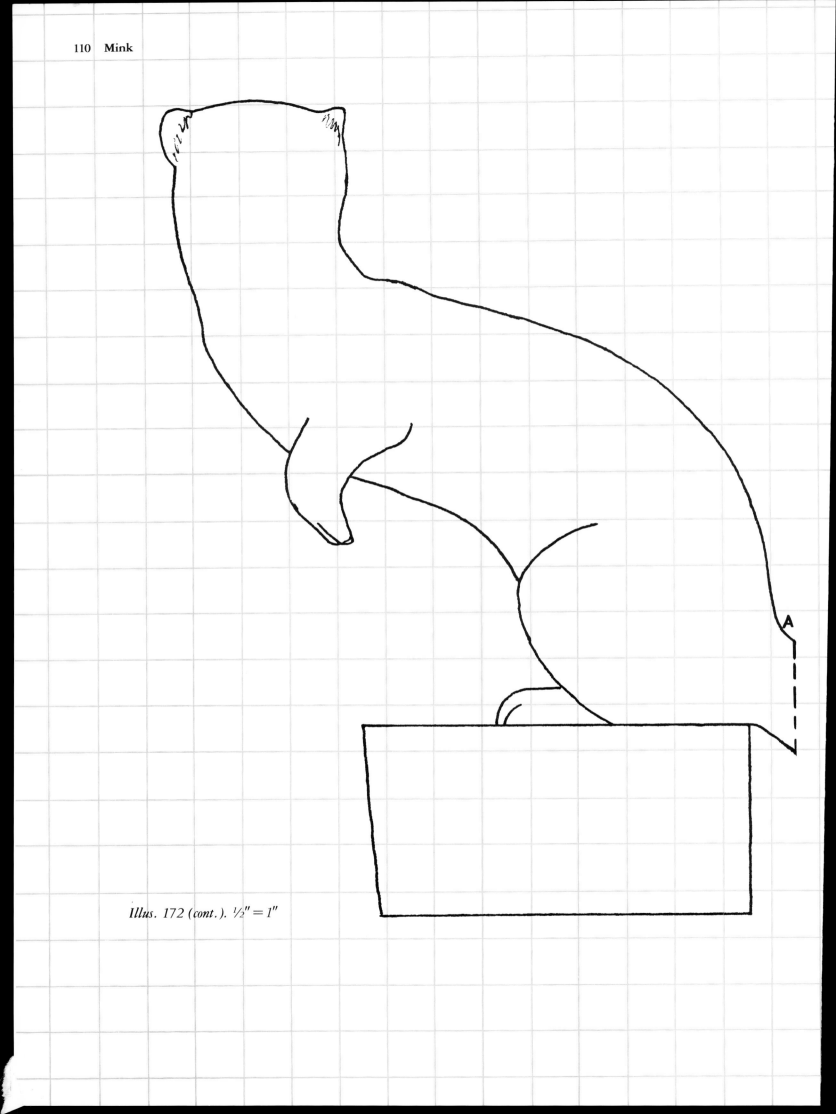

Illus. 172 (cont.). ½" = 1"

A

Illus. 172 (cont.). ½" = 1"

Wolf

The wolf looks like a German shepherd but with longer legs, larger feet and a long bushy tail—also, more powerful jaws, a wider head, and shorter ears that always stand up straight. Wolf fur is medium to light grey, with the lighter colors in southern forests. Males are larger than females and can weigh as much as 100 pounds. They can attain speeds of 20 miles per hour and sustain this speed for hours at a time.

Four to six pups are born 2 months after mating (sometime between April and May) in a den dug in the earth. They are about a week old before they can see. The parents supply both food and training to the pups. Most packs are made up of family units. When the pack travels the individual wolves keep track of each other by howling.

Man has almost wiped out the wolf by putting a bounty on his head. But in truth, the wolf is very beneficial in culling out sick or injured deer, moose, and caribou.

Illus. 173. A wolf head on an unfinished lodgepole pine log. It will be used to decorate a log building.

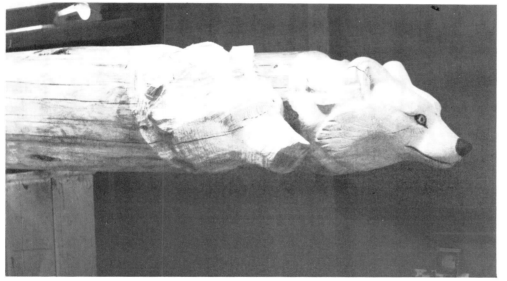

Illus. 174. Comparison of the chainsaw "rough-out" and the finished carving.

Illus. 175. Side-view of "rough-out."

Illus. 176. Top view of the "rough-out."

Illus. 177. Bottom view of the "rough-out."

Illus. 178. Shape roughed out.

Illus. 179. Wolf head close-up. Details are woodburned. Some tool marks remain to simulate a textured look.

Illus. 180. Wolf heads being placed into the structure of a log lodge.

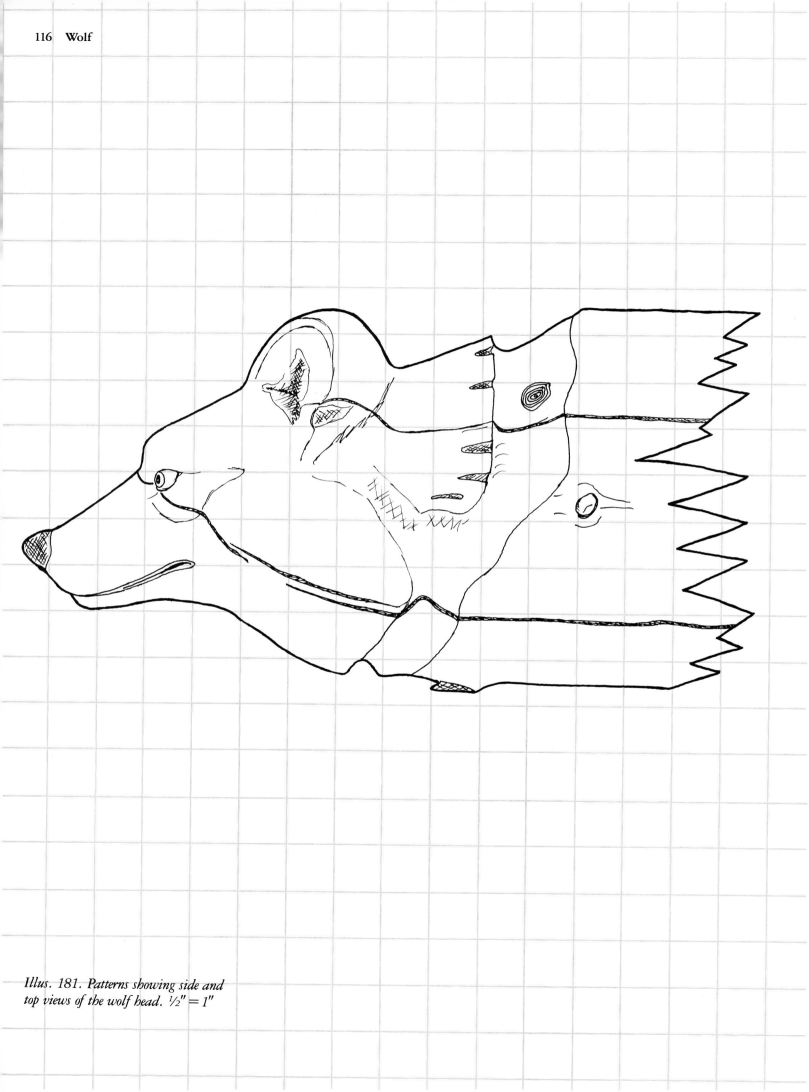

Illus. 181. Patterns showing side and top views of the wolf head. ½" = 1"

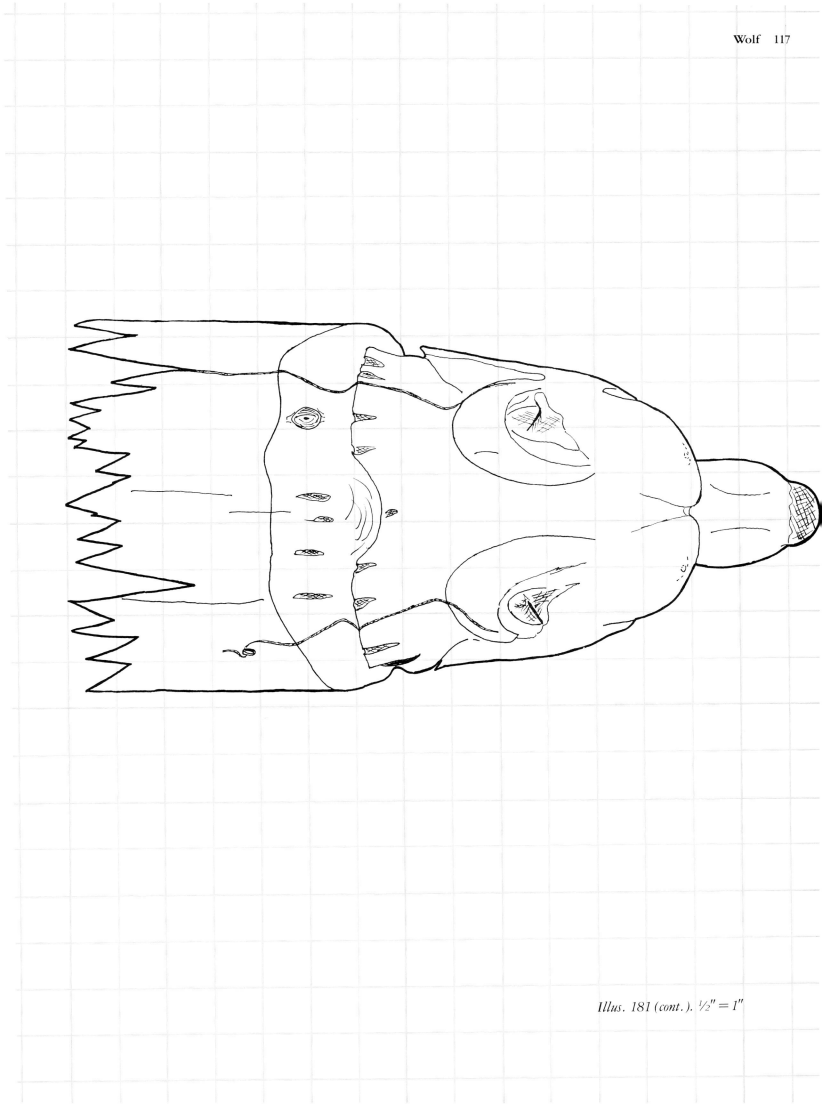

Illus. 181 (cont.). ½″ = 1″

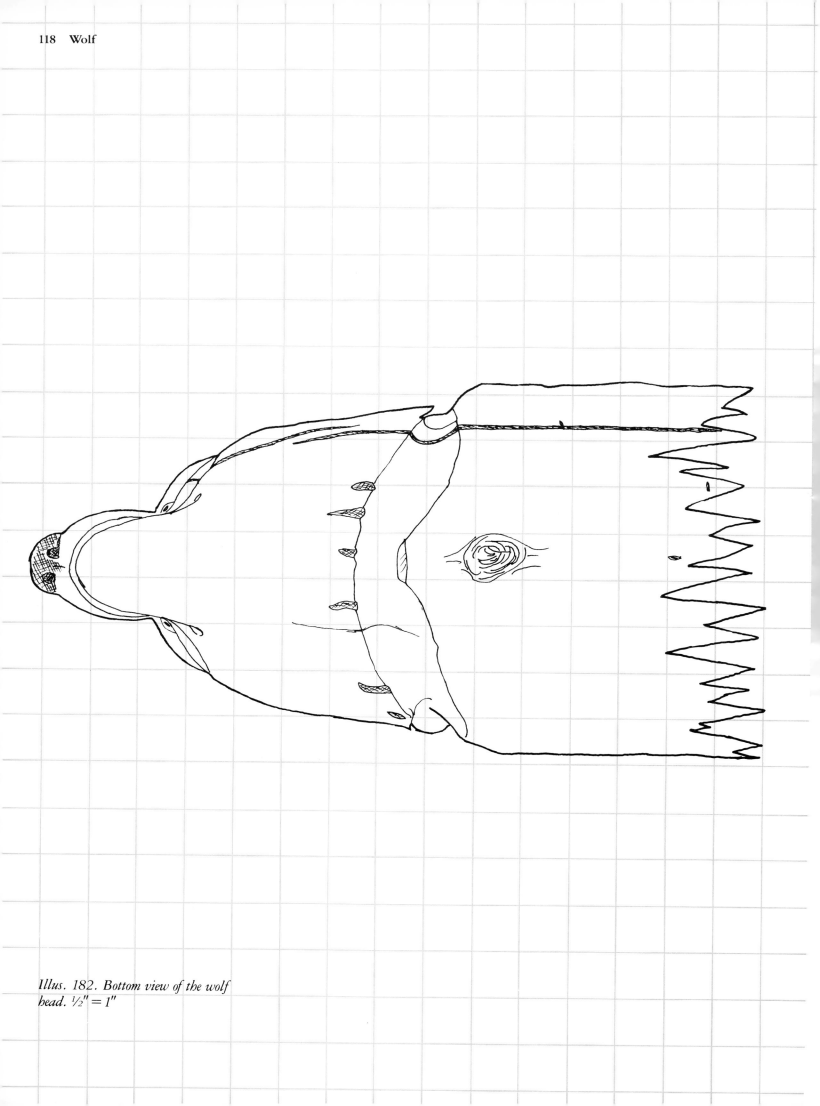

Illus. 182. Bottom view of the wolf head. ½″ = 1″

Illus. 183. Howling wolf is carved from wormy butternut log.

Illus. 184 and 185. Side views.

Illus. 186 and 187. Front and rear views.

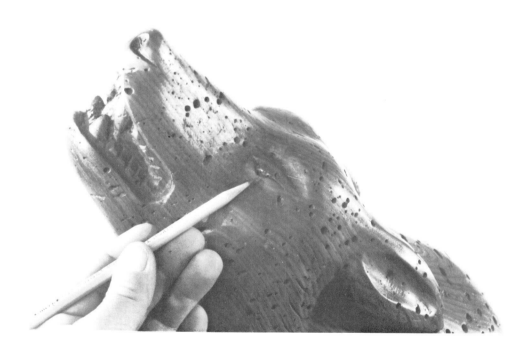

Illus. 188. V-parting tool was used to make this eye look almost closed.

Illus. 189. Shapes of the tail and rear of the howling wolf. Note the dark streak above, which is a bark seam (crack).

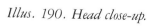

Illus. 190. Head close-up.

Illus. 191. A look into the mouth of the howling wolf.

Illus. 192. Howling wolf side views.
¼" = 1"

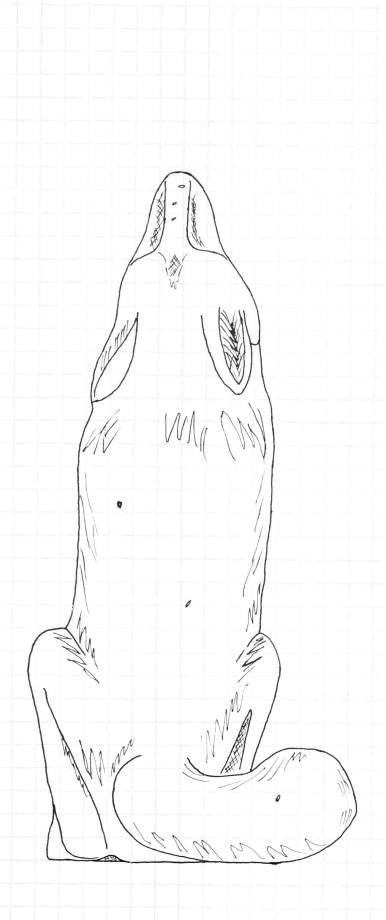

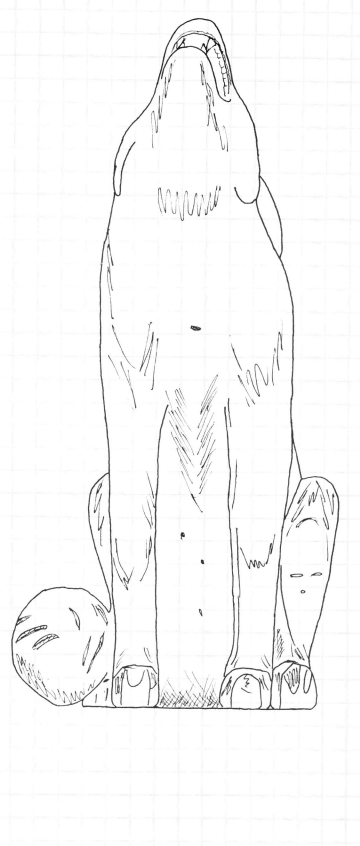

Illus. 193. Howling wolf rear and front views. ¼" = 1"

Black Bear

Male black bears weigh about 250–400 pounds. The females are about 20 percent less. Their color is usually black, but they are known to have cinnamon or brown coats. They sometimes have a white patch on their chests. Bears are plantigrade, which means they walk on the soles of their feet. The toes have five sharp curved claws. They are good climbers and fast runners, with a speed of up to 30 miles per hour.

A litter of 2 to 3 cubs is born in late winter, measuring about 6–8 inches in length. Black bears are omnivorous and have a fondness for sweets. In the winter, bears are dormant but do not hibernate.

They have a good sense of smell and hearing but poor vision. When pressed, the black bear has been known to attack but has a timid nature and tries to avoid man. They like to live in forests and swamps, are mostly nocturnal and can live and hide in woods close to man's habitation.

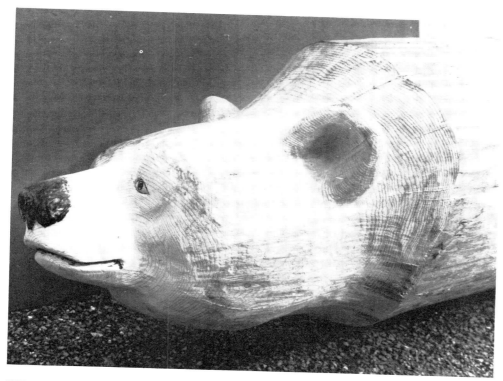

Illus. 194. Black bear head to be used horizontally is carved from a lodgepole pine log. A pair of these will be used as inside decorative extensions in a log home.

Illus. 195. Side view.

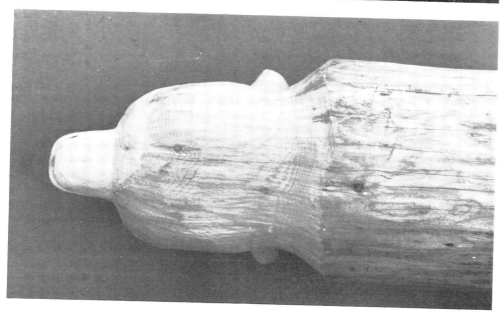

Illus. 196. Bottom view.

Illus. 197. Top view.

Illus. 198. Front view.

Illus. 199. The die grinder with structured carbide bit smoothes away chain-saw roughness, but leaves a "fur look" on the surface.

Illus. 200. Burning the nose.

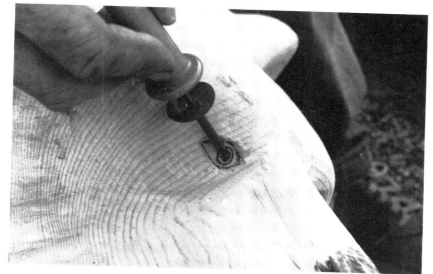

Illus. 201. Burning eye detail.

Illus. 202. The pair of carved log heads.

Illus. 203. Bear head in place, extending to the inside of a log building under construction.

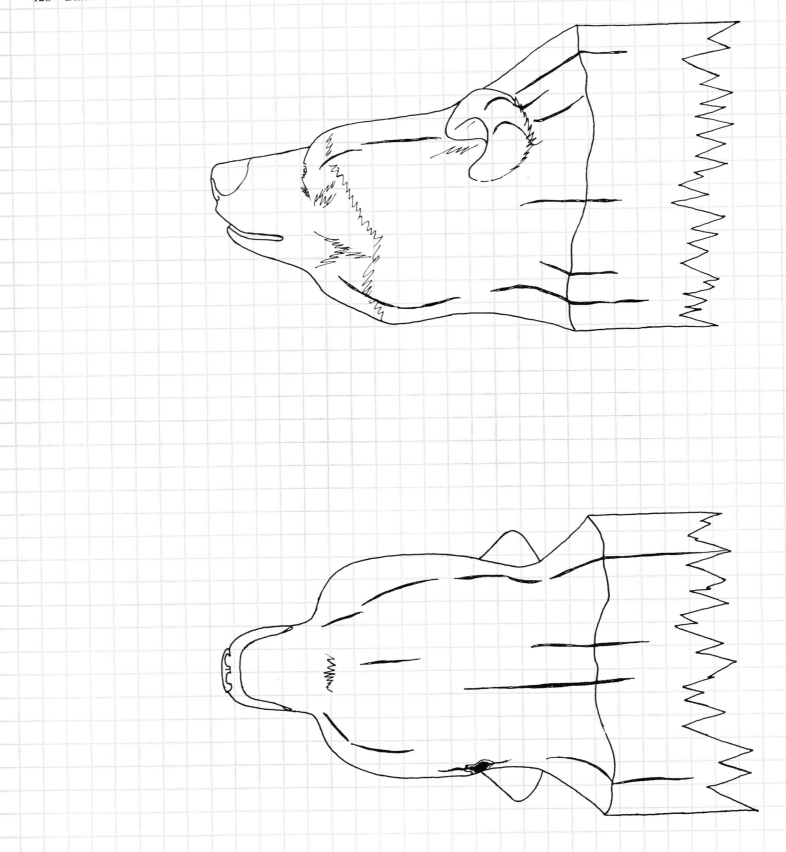

*Illus. 204. Patterns showing various
views of the black bear head (horizontal). 1/4" = 1"*

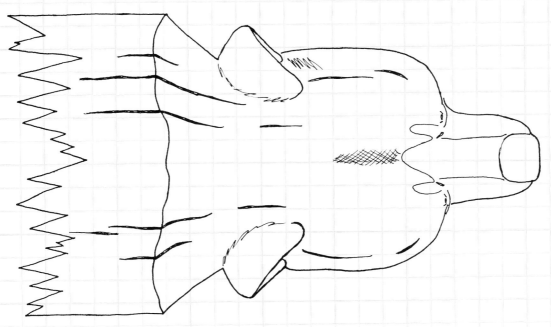

Illus. 204 (cont.). ¼″ = 1″

Illus. 205. Pattern showing front view of the black bear head (horizontal). ¼″ = 1″

Illus. 206. Bear head in the vertical position. This one is carved from lodgepole pine.

Illus. 208. Front view "in the rough."

Illus. 207. The rough and finished black bear heads.

Illus. 210. A front view of the black bear head.

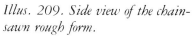

Illus. 209. Side view of the chain-sawn rough form.

Illus. 211. Side view of the black bear head.

*Illus. 212. Patterns showing various
views of the black bear head in the
vertical position.* ½" = 1"

Illus. 212 (cont.). ½″ = 1″

Illus. 212 (cont.). ½" = 1"

Illus. 212 (cont.). $\frac{1}{2}'' = 1''$

Illus. 213. Black bear cub is a one-piece carving of white cedar.

Illus. 214. Side view.

Illus. 215. Side view. Note chain-sawn sculpturing of the base.

Illus. 216. Front view of black bear cub.

Illus. 217. Rear view of black bear cub.

Illus. 218. Rough-sawn side view.

Illus. 219. Rough-cut side view.

Illus. 220. Front view of the roughed-out carving of the bear cub.

Illus. 221. Rear view. An unusually interesting piece of white cedar was used.

Illus. 222. Staining the bear with a dark walnut, transparent oil stain.

Illus. 223. An ultra close-up look at the front paws.

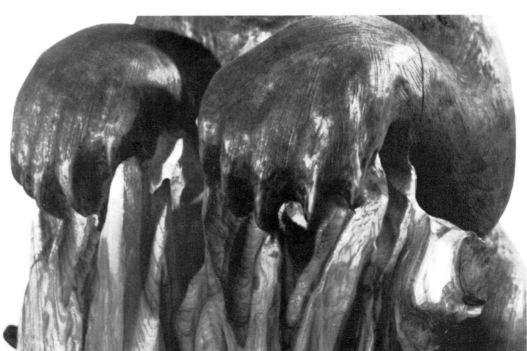

Illus. 224. Note how the bear and base appear to be joined but are actually one solid piece.

Illus. 225. This illustrates the details of the head and front paws.

Illus. 226. A forward look at the eyes and nose. Eyes were woodburned.

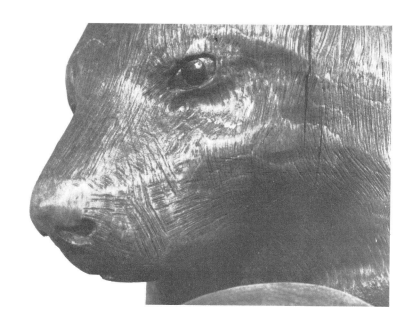

Illus. 227. Close-up shows the eye and nose detailing.

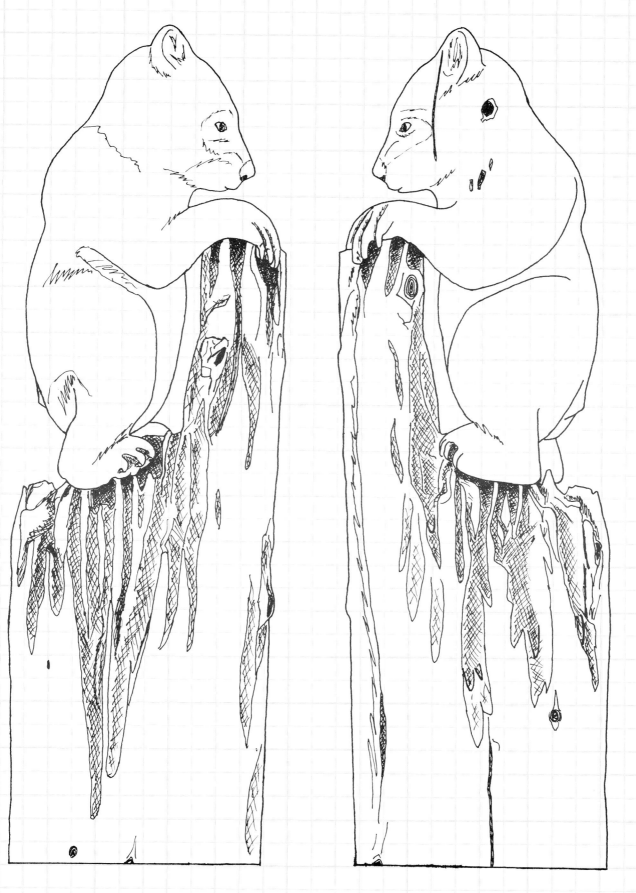

Illus. 228. Patterns showing two
side views of the black bear cub.
¼" = 1"

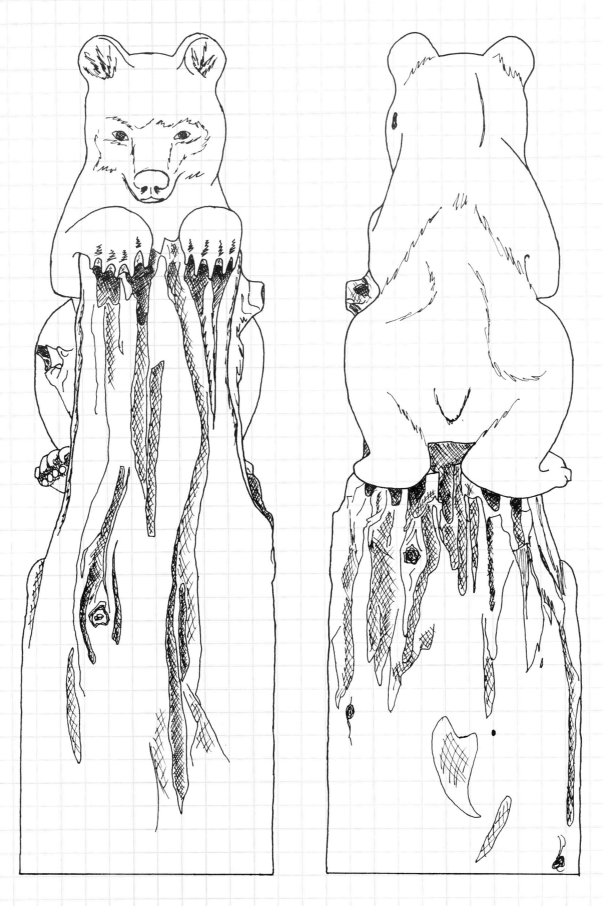

*Illus. 229. Patterns showing front
and back views of the black bear cub.*
$\frac{1}{4}" = 1"$

Raccoon

Raccoons weigh about 15 pounds with lengths of up to 3 feet, although a few may exceed this. Their forefeet resemble human hands and are very dexterous.

Raccoons are mostly nocturnal and omnivorous. They eat more food in the fall in order to build up body fat in preparation for winter dormancy and are fond of sweet or field corn.

Raccoons are good climbers and often take to trees when chased by dogs. They have been known to drown a dog in water by climbing on top of its head.

They average a life-span of up to 10 years. There are about 4 born to a litter.

Illus. 230. Small raccoon carved into a crooked butternut log, ready for finishing.

Illus. 231. A side view of the small raccoon. This carving was completed with a combination of hand gouges and electric die-grinder tooling.

Illus. 232. Woodburning the nose.

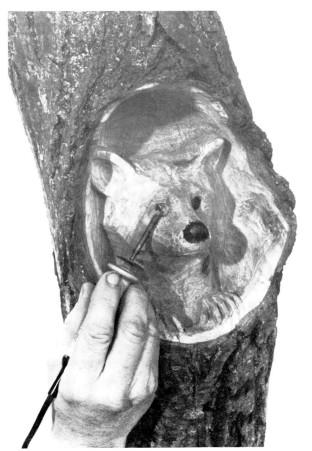

Illus. 233. Woodburning the eyes.

Illus. 234. A close-up illustrates the head in relief with woodburned detailing.

Illus. 235. Top end of the log was cut this way with a chain saw and smoothed with gouges.

Illus. 236. Apply dark oil to the raccoon and natural oil to the bark and the rest of the log.

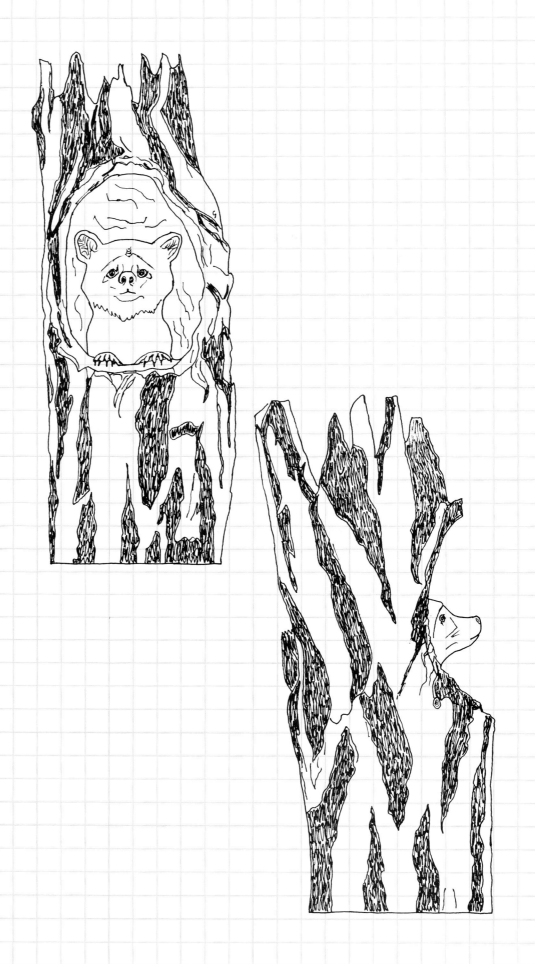

Illus. 237. Patterns for small raccoon in the log. ¼" = 1"

Illus. 238. Another raccoon carving is this raccoon family. It is relief-carved in a piece of 2-inch-thick white cedar. The top was broken before carving was started. Note the texture created with a gouge.

Illus. 239. Close-up of mother raccoon showing woodburned eyes, nose and fur.

Illus. 240. A one-piece white cedar log was used to create this full-size raccoon.

Illus. 242. Another side view.

Illus. 241. Raccoon side view. A chain saw was used to separate tail from base and to rough out the leg area as well as the overall contours.

Illus. 243. Front view.

Illus. 244. Raccoon rear view.

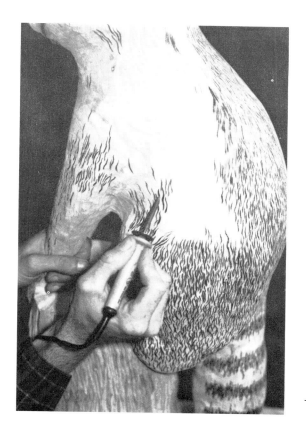

Illus. 245. Woodburning the body hairs. Each hair strand should be slightly curved. Try to achieve a uniform density with less concentration on undersides.

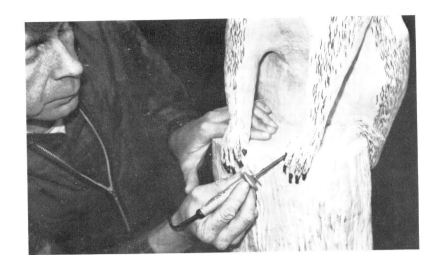

Illus. 246. Woodburning gives a glossy texture to the claws.

Illus. 247. Burning the individual hairs on a front leg.

Illus. 248. Woodburning the tail hairs to simulate color and texture and to emphasize the recognizable contrasting features of the raccoon's tail.

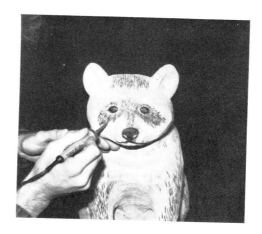

Illus. 249. Woodburning the face.

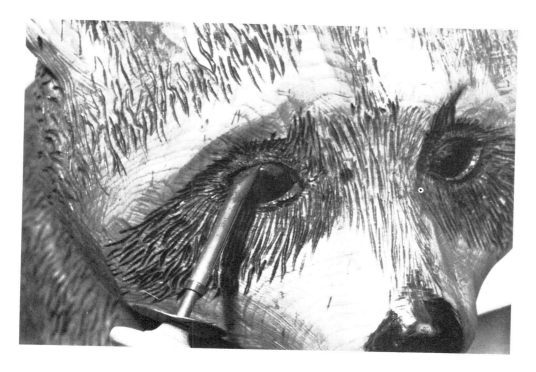

Illus. 250. Woodburning the eyes and accenting the lids.

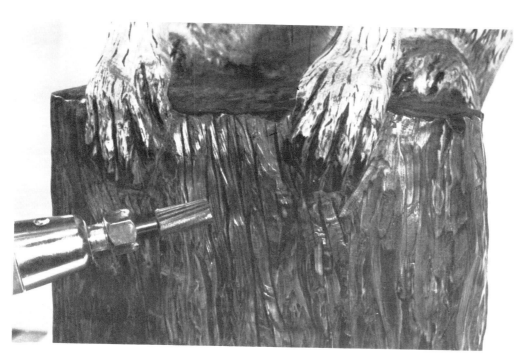

Illus. 251. A steel cutting burr is used to texture the base area to simulate a barklike look.

Illus. 252. A woodburned line, as shown, gives thickness to the bark for an additional realistic feature. A dark oil stain is then used to color the carved bark.

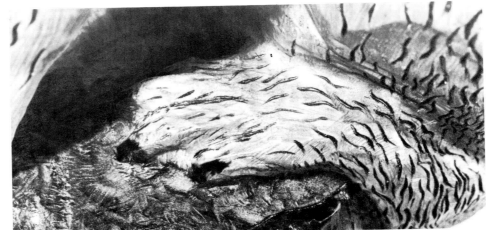

Illus. 253. This shows woodburning to the bark edge and the rear-foot claws and hairs.

Illus. 254. This crack on the back does not seriously detract from the appearance or value of the carving.

Illus. 255. A close-up look at the head. Note the glossy look of the eyes and nose.

Illus. 256. Pattern showing side view of the large raccoon. ¼" = 1"

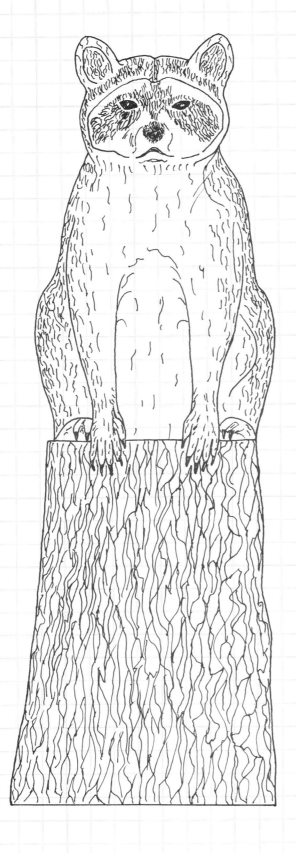
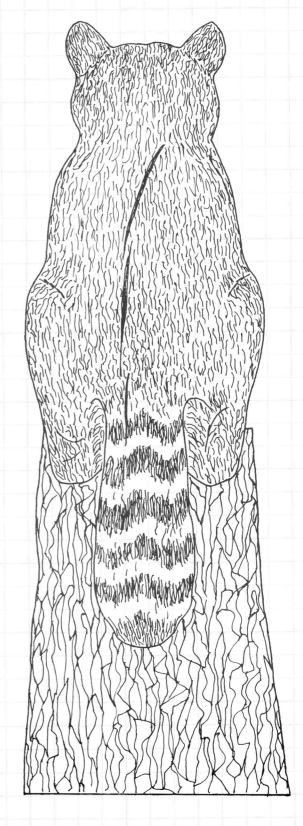

Illus. 257. Patterns showing front and rear views. ¼" = 1"

Red Fox

The red fox is about 3–3½ feet long including the tail which is about 15 inches in length. It weighs about 12 pounds, more or less. They have a lot of color variations, with a black nose, ear tips, feet, and white underparts. They are very clever and intelligent animals with very keen senses, and are excellent hunters. A big part of their diet consists of rabbits, mice, and just about any rodent.

An average of 7 or 8 kits are taken care of by both parents.

Illus. 258. Sleeping fox is carved from a large "slice" of a box elder log.

Illus. 259. This one-piece carving of the sleeping fox from another view.

Illus. 260 and 261. Back views.

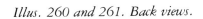

Illus. 262 and 263. More back views of the sleeping fox.

Illus. 264. View of facial detail of fox.

Illus. 265. View showing the shape of the head, leg and tail.

Illus. 266. Top view of sleeping fox. Raw wood on carved surfaces of base was stained to match the rest of base.

Illus. 267. Roughing out the basic shape with the chain saw.

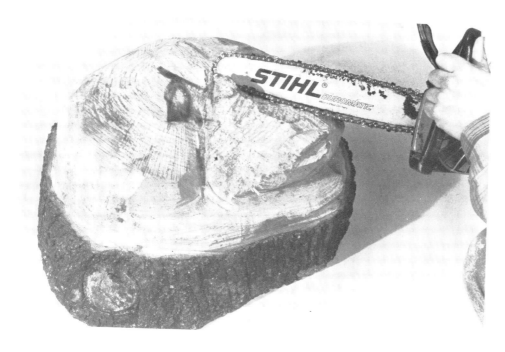

Illus. 268. Shaping the neck and ears.

Illus. 269. The chain-saw roughing work completed.

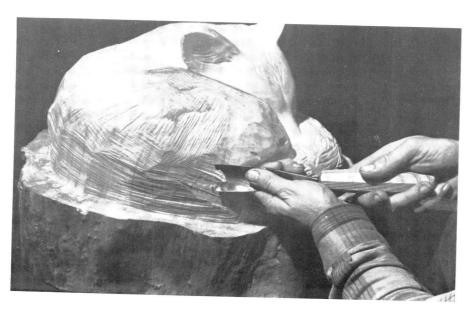

Illus. 270. With the bark carved away, the big gouge is used for initial smoothing.

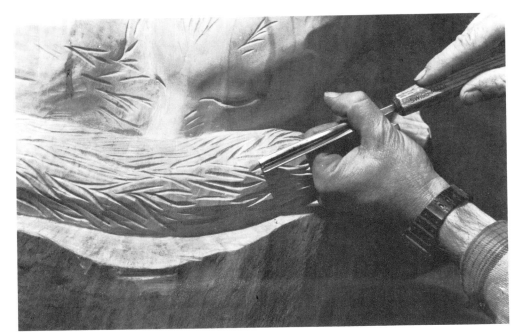

Illus. 271. Using the V-parting tool to texture the tail.

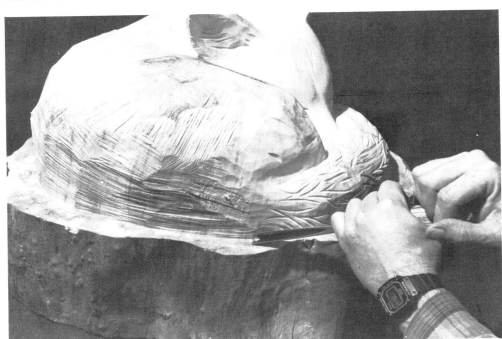

Illus. 272. Defining the animal and the base separation with a V-parting tool.

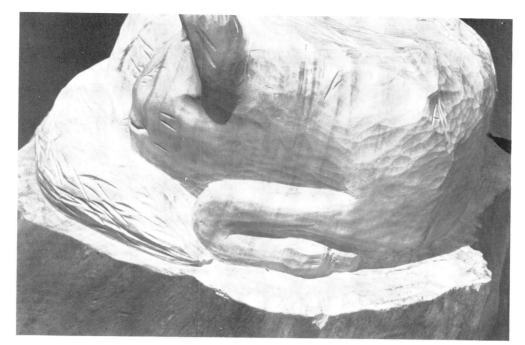

Illus. 273. A close-up look at the curled leg and tail.

Illus. 274. Ready for staining and finishing.

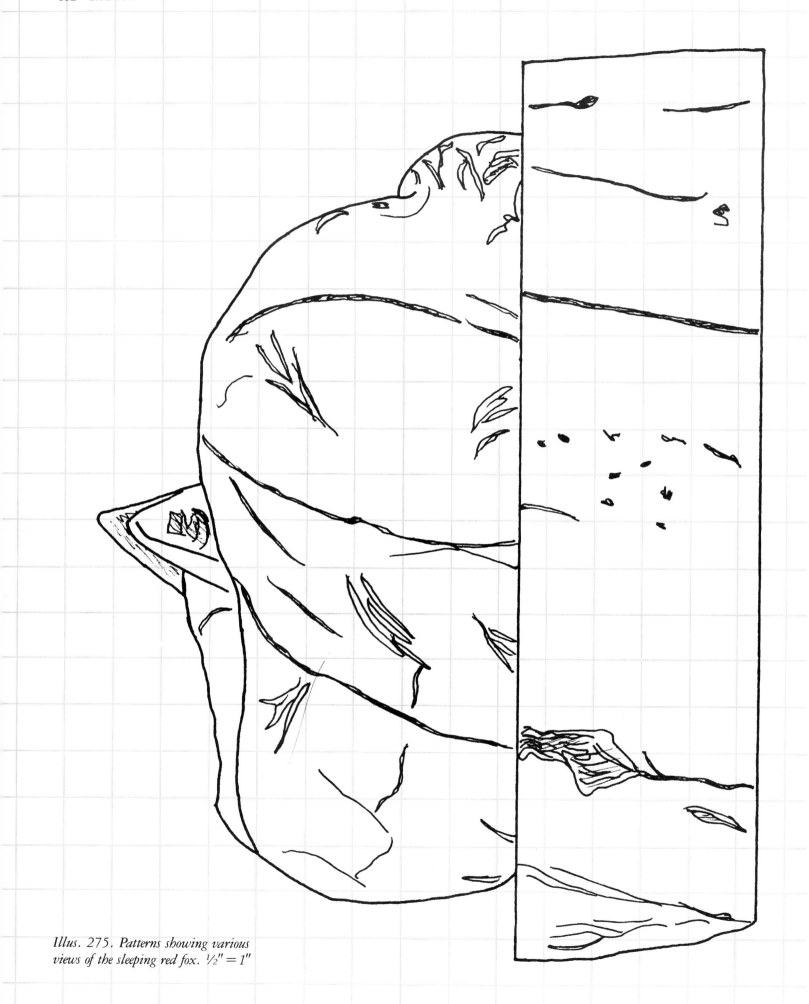

*Illus. 275. Patterns showing various
views of the sleeping red fox.* ½" = 1"

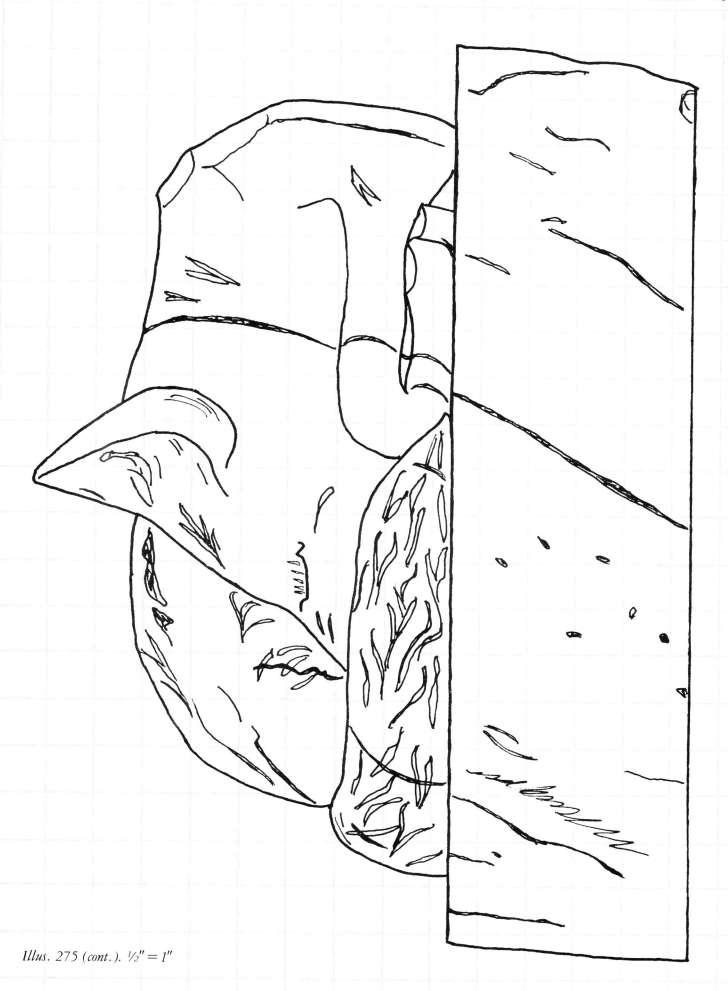

Illus. 275 (cont.). ½″ = 1″

Illus. 275 (cont.). ½″ = 1″

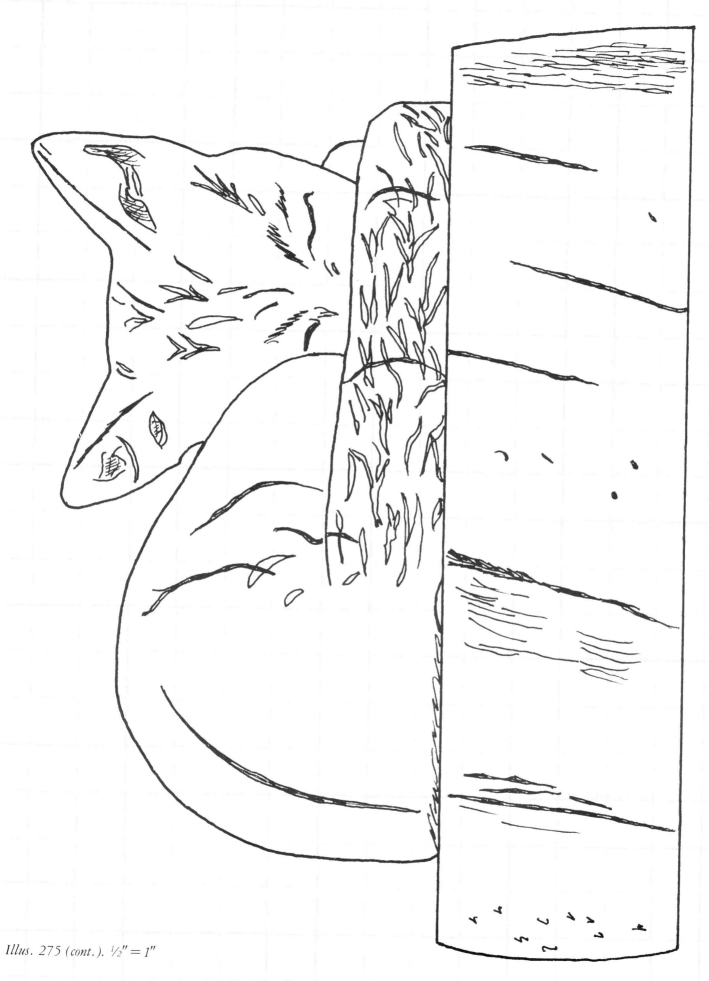

Illus. 275 (cont.). ½″ = 1″

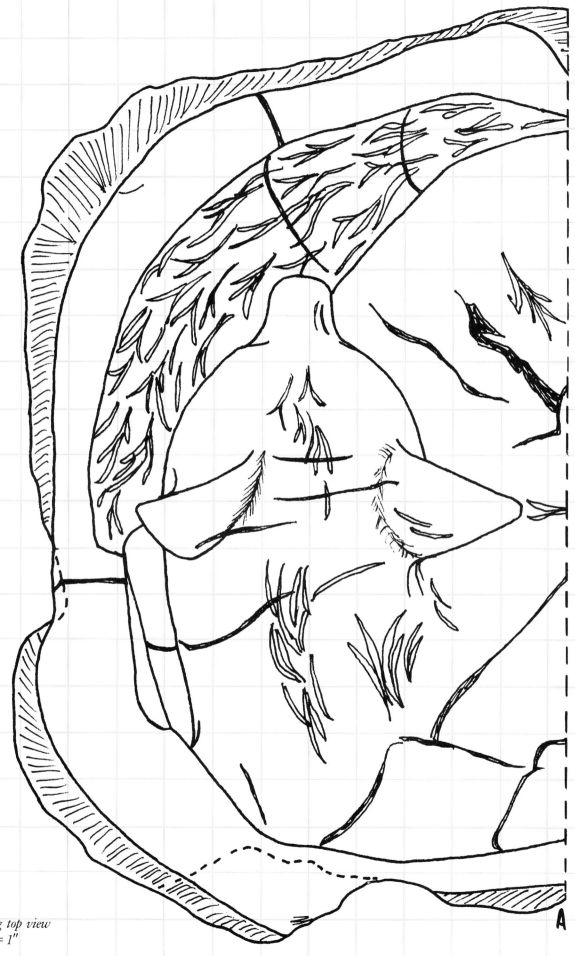

*Illus. 276. Pattern showing top view
of the sleeping red fox. ½" = 1"*

A

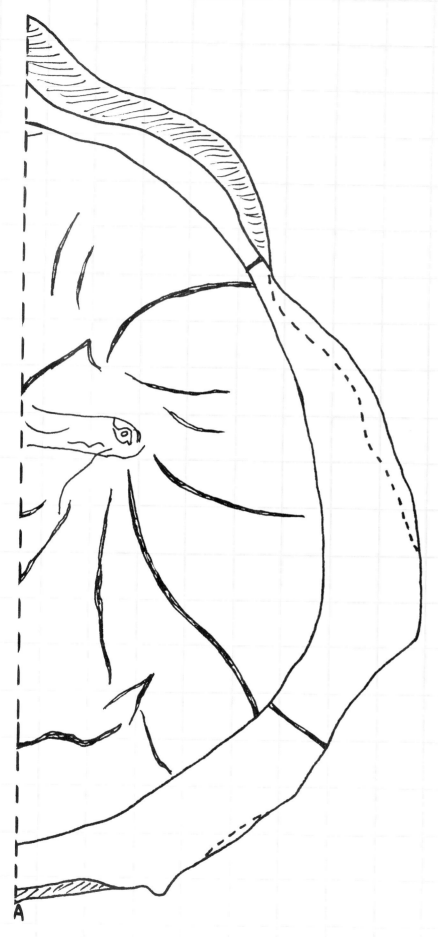

Illus. 276 (cont.). ½″ = 1″

Illus. 277. The stalking red fox is carved from a black cherry log.

Illus. 278. A closer look at the forward body details from the opposite side. The wild or black cherry wood used for this carving has an exceptionally rich, red color, but it tends to crack.

Illus. 279. One side view of the stalking fox.

Illus. 280. Another side view.

Illus. 281. Top view.

Illus. 282. Bottom view. Carving was planned so that major crack(s) would be to the bottom, as shown.

Illus. 283. Head details.

Illus. 284. Tail-texturing can be done with a rasp, gouge, or rotary tool.

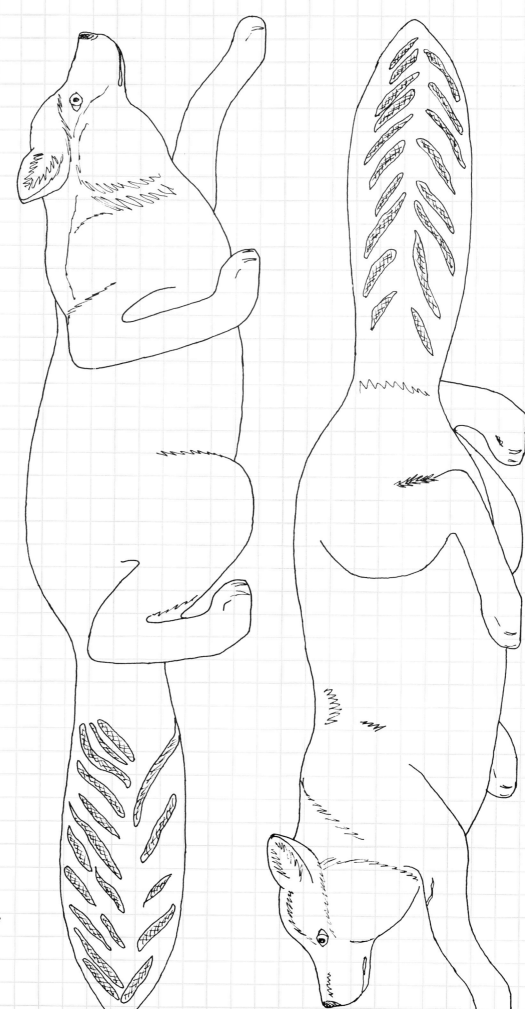

*Illus. 285. Patterns showing three
views of the stalking red fox.*
$\frac{1}{4}'' = 1''$

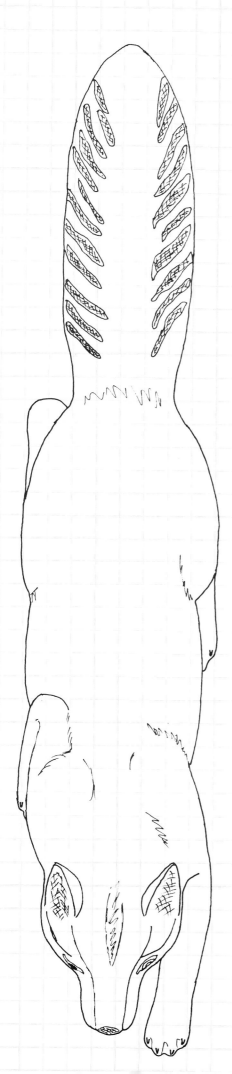

Illus. 286. Pattern showing front view of the stalking red fox. ¼" = 1"

Illus. 285 (cont.). ¼" = 1"

Badger

B.D.

Badgers are members of the weasel family. They live underground, eating mice, gophers, ground squirrels, and other small animals dug out with their powerful front claws. Because of their short legs, they waddle when walking and look clumsy when running. They are silver-grey, about 2 feet long and have wide bodies with short necks and flat heads, with a white stripe that runs between the eyes onto the back.

The badger hunts by night and sleeps by day. If approached, away from its den, it will run and hide, but if cornered, will fight savagely and courageously.

The young are born in April to early June. The annual litter size is 1–5, with 2 or 3 as an average. They are born with eyes closed and almost hairless. The mother feeds the young until early fall, when they are on their own.

Illus. 287. The badger is carved from a solid chunk of butternut. Features are accentuated with woodburning and bleaching.

Illus. 288. A side view.

Illus. 289. Bottom view of the badger. Note the hollowing out of material to minimize the possibility of cracking.

Illus. 290. The chain-sawn "rough out," ready for further shaping.

Illus. 291. Side view in the rough.

Illus. 292. The rough, chain-sawn top view. The knot visible here will be subdued later with bleach.

Illus. 293. Deep body-texturing is achieved with the chain saw.

Illus. 294. Nostrils and mouth are cut with a narrow gouge.

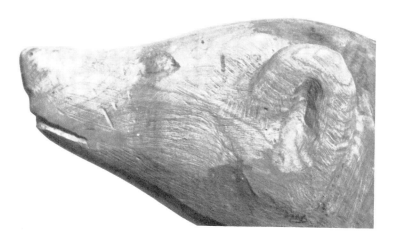

Illus. 295. The initial steps of detailing the head.

Illus. 296. Shaping is completed. The carving is ready for finishing and special effects.

Illus. 297. A torch is used to slightly char the darker areas of the badger.

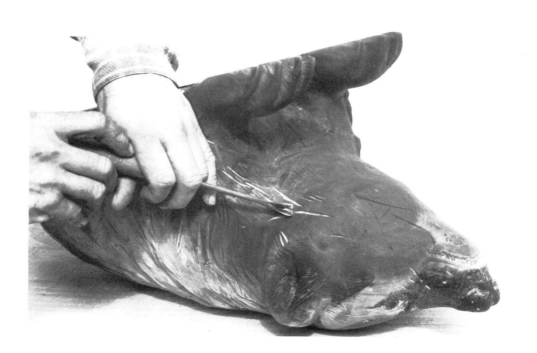

Illus. 298. Randomly cutting through the charred surface, as shown, gives a highlighting look by breaking up the total dark effect.

Illus. 299. Texturing and high-lighting can be done with a rotary tool and a sharp burr.

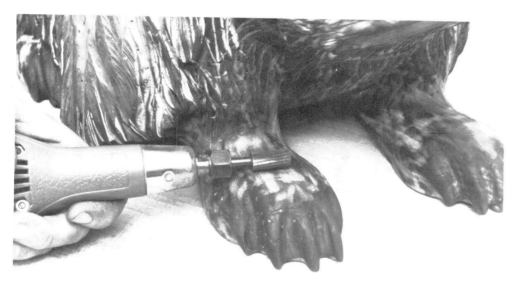

Illus. 300. Another technique of highlighting uses the side of the rotary burr to cut through, or partly through, the torch-charred areas.

Illus. 301. Bleaching: Applying the first component (A).

Illus. 302. Bleaching: Apply the second solution (B).

Illus. 303. Starting the "shaggy hair" look, typical of the badger, is done with the burning tool.

Illus. 304. The thick, shaggy-hair look emerges when woodburning hairs on the carved and bleached surface.

Illus. 305. The flat bevel of the woodburning tool is used to "color" the head.

Illus. 306. All texturing, bleaching and woodburning is completed. The final step is to apply a natural oil finish.

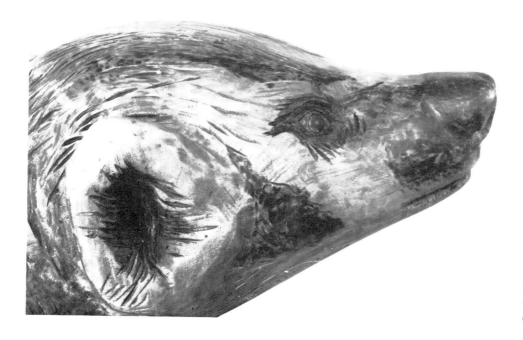

Illus. 307. A close-up look at the badger head. Note the simply formed ears.

Illus. 308. Rear foot of the badger.

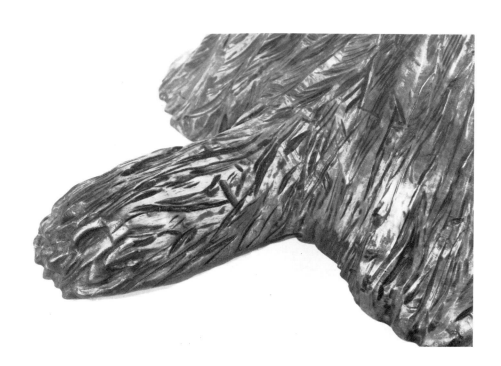

Illus. 309. The finished badger tail.

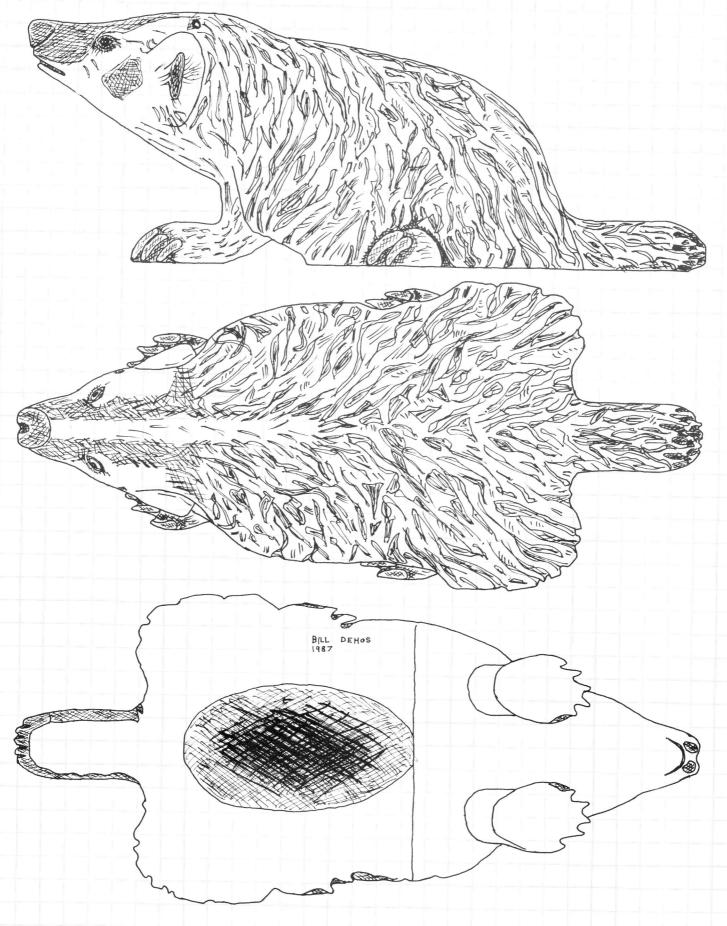

BILL DEHOS
1987

*Illus. 310. Patterns showing three
views of the badger.* ¼″ = 1″

Illus. 311. Pattern showing front view. ¼″ = 1″

Whitetail Deer (Fawn)

Whitetail deer are common in most of the United States and southern Canada.

In warm weather they have reddish-brown hair, in winter, greyish-brown. Their average weight is about 150 pounds. Deer have an acute sense of smell and good hearing, but are color-blind. They eat most forms of vegetation. Deer can attain speeds of up to 40 miles per hour.

A doe will have 1, 2, or sometimes 3 fawns, each weighing about 5 pounds. The fawns have spotted coats, an extremely good camouflage.

Dogs are more of a threat to deer than wild animals. Deer are very adaptable and are often overpopulated at times.

Illus. 312. Fawn of solid butternut is carved from two pieces. The head is attached to the body in decoy fashion.

Illus. 313. Here's how the body and head pieces should be taken from the log. The joint (with dowel reinforcement) will be less conspicuous because the joining members are from the same part of the log.

Illus. 314. A bottom view of the rough-carved body. Note the hollowing to minimize the possible cracking.

Illus. 315. View of the roughed-out head.

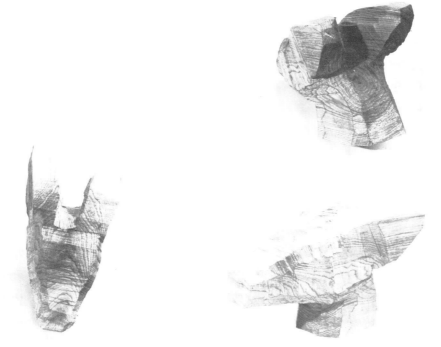

Illus. 316. A back view of the roughed-out head.

Illus. 317. Left: A forward look at the roughed-out head.

Illus. 318. Right: The head as chain-sawn in the rough.

Illus. 319. If possible, level the gluing surface on the jointer, as shown.

Illus. 320. Boring the dowel hole. A level check assures that the hole will be perpendicular to the glue joint surface.

Illus. 321. Once the head is supported level with shims and blocking, bore the hole.

Illus. 322. Looking at the head from still another view. Note the dowel hole.

Illus. 323. The roughed-out body and head pieces.

Illus. 324. Looking at the roughed-out head. Note the preliminary cut, locating the eye. Head is temporarily attached at this point to complete the rough shaping.

Illus. 325. A side view shows the completion of the chain-sawn roughing-out operation.

Illus. 326. Using a spoon gouge to contour the concave surface inside the ear.

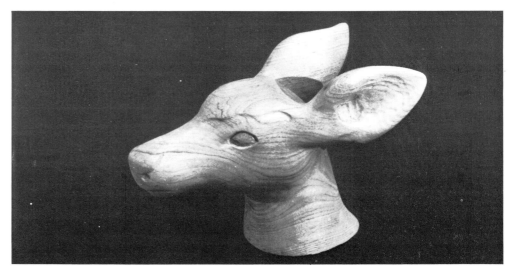

Illus. 327. Shaping is almost complete, ready for final detailing.

Illus. 328. The head worked a little further along. Note the hollowing of the ear.

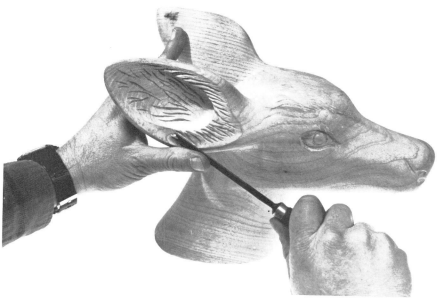

Illus. 329. Making some cuts to simulate hair.

Illus. 330. Making some cuts to simulate hair on the brow or forehead.

Illus. 331. The head with all carving and shaping completed, ready for woodburning details.

Illus. 332. The head with woodburned nose and eyes.

Illus. 333. Bleaching the spots typical on a young fawn. Note the bleached areas around the eyes and ears. Solution A brings the pigments of the wood to the surface. This will be followed by an application of solution B, which is required to turn the wood lighter.

Illus. 334. Bleaching along the edges of the tail, results in the "white-tail" effect.

Illus. 335. Lastly, apply natural oil, followed with wax. The natural tan of the butternut wood, coupled with the bleached areas and the dark woodburned details, will make a very impressive sculpture.

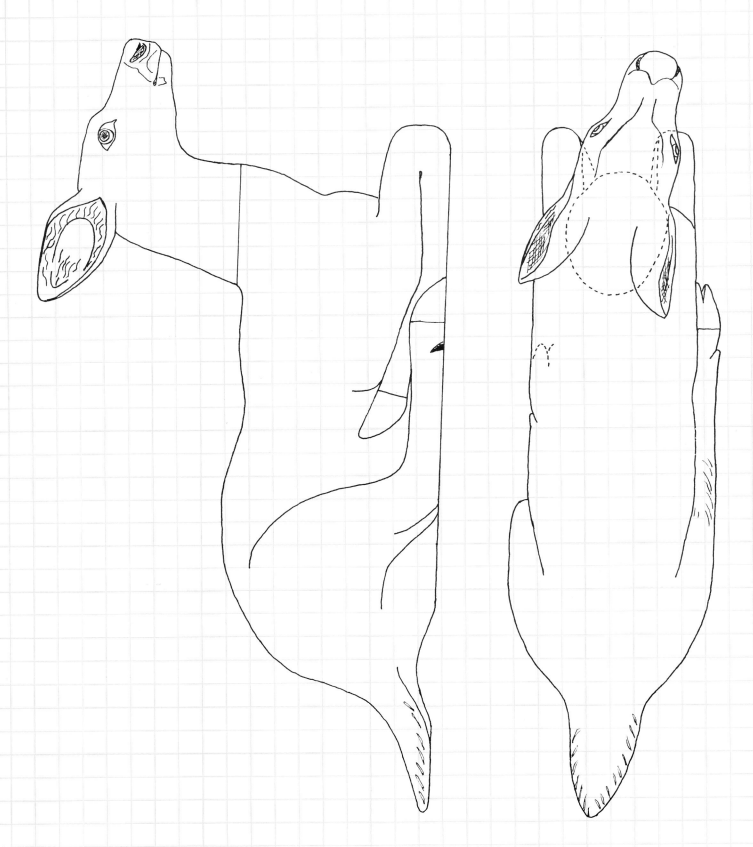

Illus. 336. Patterns, showing side and top views of the white-tail fawn.
$\frac{1}{4}'' = 1''$

Illus. 337. Patterns, showing front
and side views of the white-tail
fawn. 1/4" = 1"

Beaver

Beavers are 3–4 feet long, including their wide paddlelike tails, and weigh from 40 to 60 pounds. The fur varies from shiny dark brown to yellowish brown. Their bodies are well adapted for swimming and working underwater, possessing transparent eyelids, closable nostrils, closable flaps behind the teeth, flat tail, and webbed rear feet. Two claws on each rear foot are split and are used to comb the fur. Strong, chisel-like teeth enable them to cut down trees for food and building material. Beaver dams can be very large and strong and their lodges, places of safety. Their tails are scaly and used to slap the water's surface for warning signals.

The kits are born with their eyes open in April or May and live with their parents for 2 years.

Illus. 338. Beaver is carved of wormy butternut on a separate pine slab base.

Illus. 339. One side view of the chain-sawn, roughed-out beaver.

Illus. 340. The other side view of the roughed-out carving.

Illus. 341. A top view of the beaver in the rough.

Illus. 342. The bottom is contoured to match the curvature of the slab base.

Illus. 343. Preliminary shaping of the front incisors (teeth).

Illus. 344. Making cuts to simulate gnawing of the beaver.

Illus. 345. Final shaping and outside body-contouring is done with a disc sander.

Illus. 346. Remove cross-grain disc sander marks with a small pad sander.

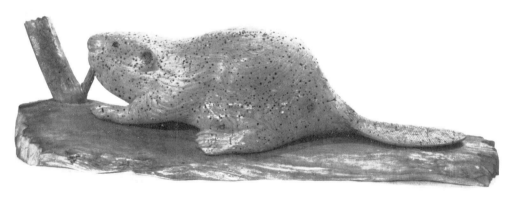

Illus. 347. A pine branch was "tailor"-selected and set into a knot-hole in the base so that a part of this branch fits against the teeth of the beaver as shown in Illus. 348.

Illus. 348. This close-up shows the twig of a branch against the teeth.

Illus. 349. A closer look at the branch inserted in the knothole of the slab base and the forward foot shape.

Illus. 350. The rear foot is webbed for swimming and should be carved, as shown.

Illus. 351. The woodburning tool textures the flat paddle-like tail, simulating a scaly look.

Illus. 352. The ends of the base are made jagged with the chain saw and smoothed by hand. A mixture of vinegar and steel wool was used to make a stain to age the fresh-cut surfaces. The mixture must set for some time, from a few hours to overnight to achieve the shade or depth of color desired.

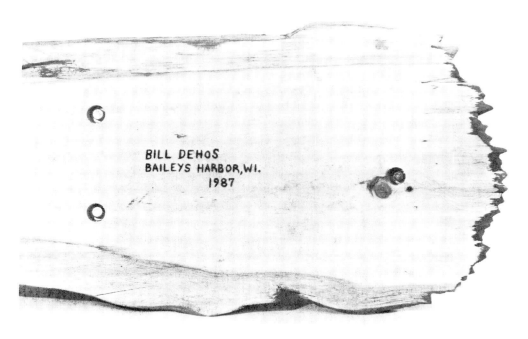

Illus. 353. This underside of the base shows the counter-bored lag-screw mounting holes, the jagged ends and the burned-in signature and date of the artist.

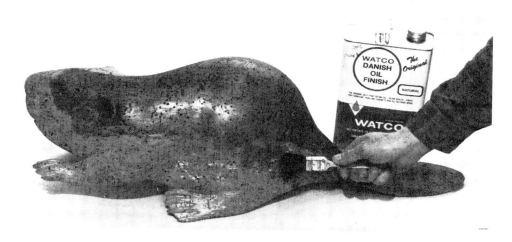

Illus. 354. A natural finish is appropriate.

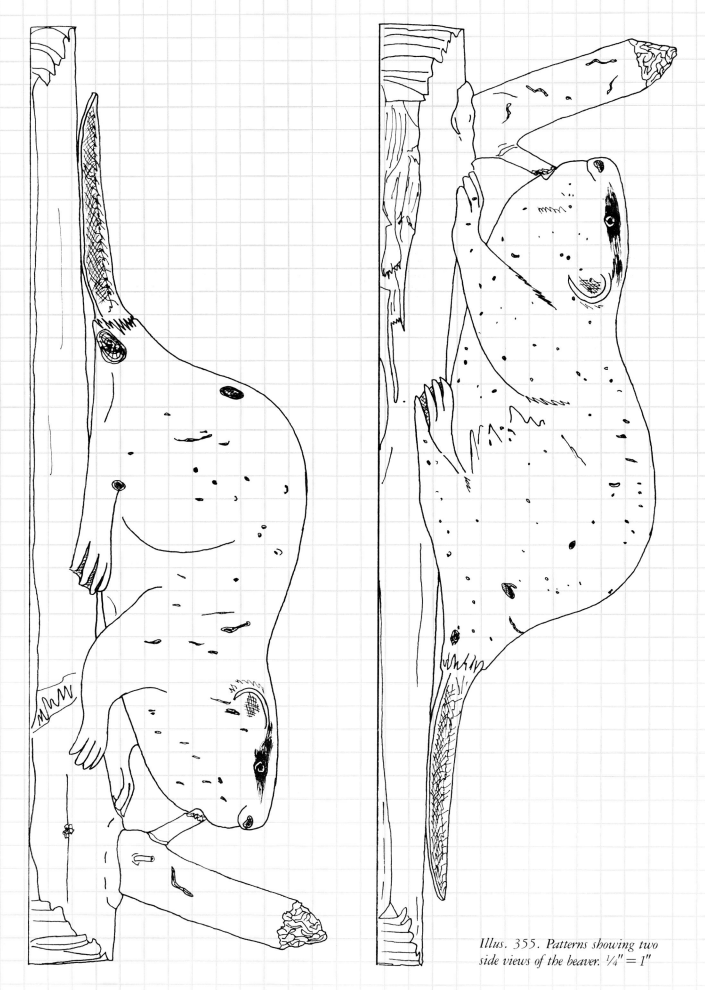

*Illus. 355. Patterns showing two
side views of the beaver. ¼" = 1"*

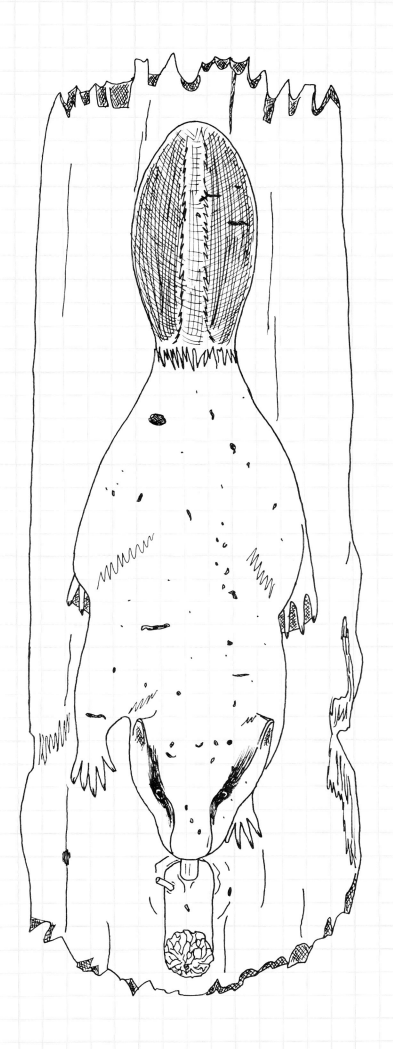

Illus. 356. Pattern showing top view of the beaver. $\frac{1}{4}$" = 1"

Cougar

Cougars when fully grown can be 4–5 feet long, not counting their 2 to 3 foot tails. They weigh up to 227 pounds. The body is slender with long legs and a head that is rather small and round. The fur is either grey or a reddish yellow color called tawny. The throat, insides of the legs, and the belly are white, and the tip of the tail is black. Sometimes cougars are completely black.

Litter size is 1 to 5 (the average is 3) cubs at a time. They are cared for by the adults until they can survive by themselves, in about two years. They can live to be 10 to 12 years old.

Cougars hunt mostly at night and can travel many miles in search of game. They prey on deer, elk, and sometimes on bighorn sheep. They also feed on small animals.

Illus. 357. This massive cougar carving of box elder is well over 6 feet in length.

Illus. 358. Looking at the upper and forward features of the cougar.

Illus. 359. A close-up showing the jaw and other head details.

Illus. 360. A side view. The body is the main trunk of the tree with the tail as a branch.

Illus. 361. A top view.

Illus. 362. The bottom.

Illus. 363. The cougar in a very rough, chain-sawn shape.

Illus. 364. Looking at the rough-cut from the top side.

Illus. 365. Working on the bottom, making a notching cut between the front feet.

Illus. 366. Roughed-out shoulder and head areas.

Illus. 367. Rounding over the tail.

Illus. 368. Starting to refine and define some of the body.

Illus. 369. One side view of the chain-sawn roughing work nearly complete.

Illus. 370. The disc sander removes the roughness remaining from the chain saw and brings the body closer to the final contour.

Illus. 371. Heavy sanding almost complete; the carving is now ready for more refined detailing.

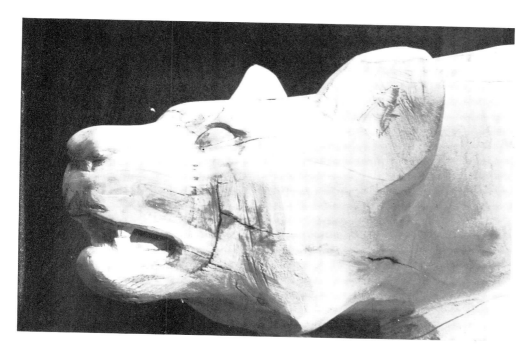

Illus. 372. Some of the preliminary detailing started.

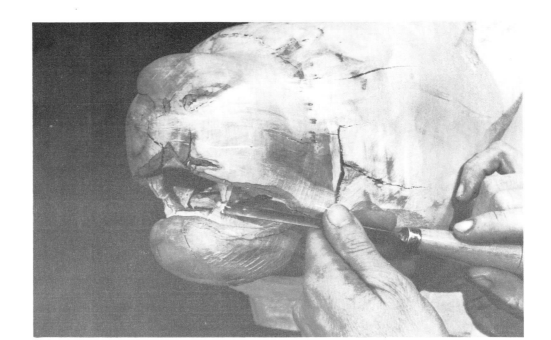

Illus. 373. Working on the mouth's line and gums with a small gouge.

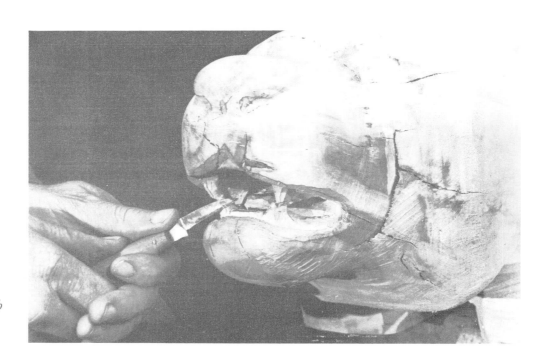

Illus. 374. Knife work is good for some of the detailing, but not for the "long reach," deeper cutting jobs, such as those required when carving well inside the mouth.

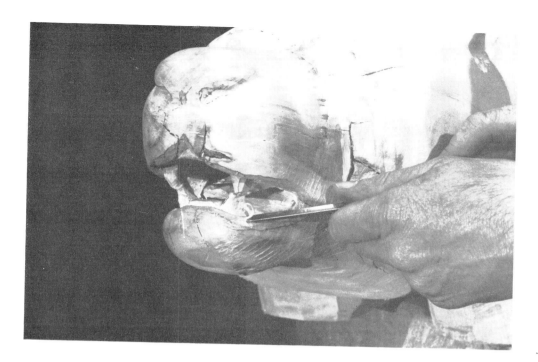

Illus. 375. *A small gouge can be used to cut the teeth.* Caution: *The teeth will have short or cross grain, which could snap off if not cut carefully.*

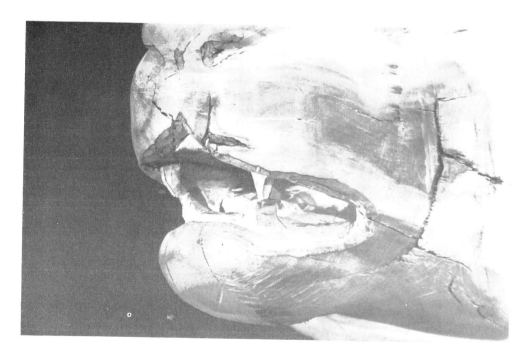

Illus. 376. *A close look at the roughly shaped teeth. Note the depth of the cavity carved inside the mouth opening.*

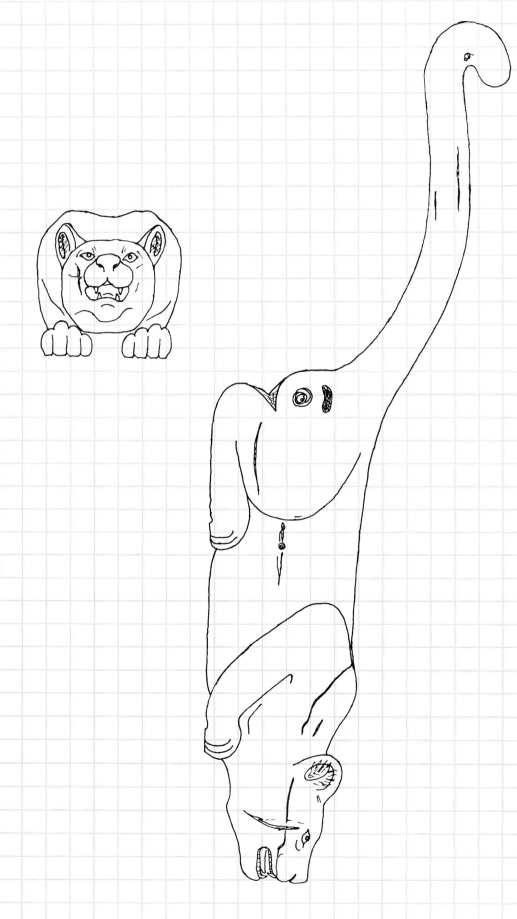

*Illus. 377. Patterns showing various
views of the cougar.* ⅛" = 1"

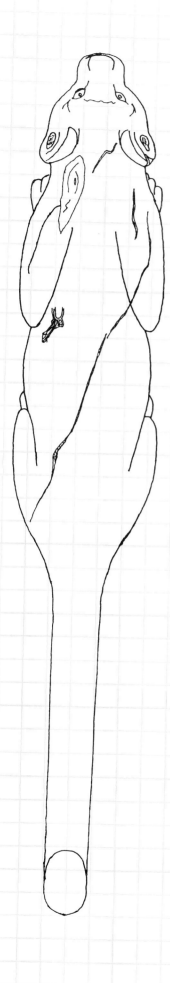
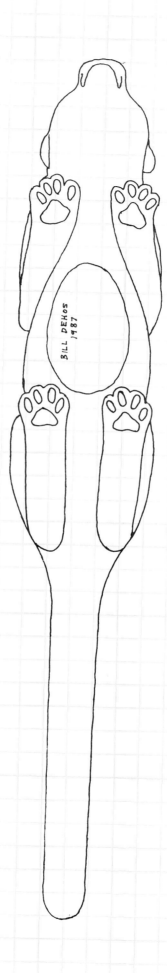

Illus. 377 (cont.). ⅛″ = 1″

APPENDICES

METRIC EQUIVALENCY CHART

MM—MILLIMETRES   CM—CENTIMETRES

INCHES TO MILLIMETRES AND CENTIMETRES

INCHES	MM	CM	INCHES	CM	INCHES	CM
⅛	3	0.3	9	22.9	30	76.2
¼	6	0.6	10	25.4	31	78.7
⅜	10	1.0	11	27.9	32	81.3
½	13	1.3	12	30.5	33	83.8
⅝	16	1.6	13	33.0	34	86.4
¾	19	1.9	14	35.6	35	88.9
⅞	22	2.2	15	38.1	36	91.4
1	25	2.5	16	40.6	37	94.0
1¼	32	3.2	17	43.2	38	96.5
1½	38	3.8	18	45.7	39	99.1
1¾	44	4.4	19	48.3	40	101.6
2	51	5.1	20	50.8	41	104.1
2½	64	6.4	21	53.3	42	106.7
3	76	7.6	22	55.9	43	109.2
3½	89	8.9	23	58.4	44	111.8
4	102	10.2	24	61.0	45	114.3
4½	114	11.4	25	63.5	46	116.8
5	127	12.7	26	66.0	47	119.4
6	152	15.2	27	68.6	48	121.9
7	178	17.8	28	71.1	49	124.5
8	203	20.3	29	73.7	50	127.0

YARDS TO METRES

YARDS	METRES	YARDS	METRES	YARDS	METRES	YARDS	METRES	YARDS	METRES
⅛	0.11	2⅛	1.94	4⅛	3.77	6⅛	5.60	8⅛	7.43
¼	0.23	2¼	2.06	4¼	3.89	6¼	5.72	8¼	7.54
⅜	0.34	2⅜	2.17	4⅜	4.00	6⅜	5.83	8⅜	7.66
½	0.46	2½	2.29	4½	4.11	6½	5.94	8½	7.77
⅝	0.57	2⅝	2.40	4⅝	4.23	6⅝	6.06	8⅝	7.89
¾	0.69	2¾	2.51	4¾	4.34	6¾	6.17	8¾	8.00
⅞	0.80	2⅞	2.63	4⅞	4.46	6⅞	6.29	8⅞	8.12
1	0.91	3	2.74	5	4.57	7	6.40	9	8.23
1⅛	1.03	3⅛	2.86	5⅛	4.69	7⅛	6.52	9⅛	8.34
1¼	1.14	3¼	2.97	5¼	4.80	7¼	6.63	9¼	8.46
1⅜	1.26	3⅜	3.09	5⅜	4.91	7⅜	6.74	9⅜	8.57
1½	1.37	3½	3.20	5½	5.03	7½	6.86	9½	8.69
1⅝	1.49	3⅝	3.31	5⅝	5.14	7⅝	6.97	9⅝	8.80
1¾	1.60	3¾	3.43	5¾	5.26	7¾	7.09	9¾	8.92
1⅞	1.71	3⅞	3.54	5⅞	5.37	7⅞	7.20	9⅞	9.03
2	1.83	4	3.66	6	5.49	8	7.32	10	9.14

ABOUT THE AUTHORS

Patrick Spielman's love of wood began when, as a child, he transformed fruit crates into toys. Now this prolific and innovative woodworker is respected worldwide as a teacher and author.

His most famous contribution to the woodworking field has been his perfection of a method to season green wood with polyethylene glycol 1000 (PEG). He went on to invent, manufacture, and distribute the PEG-Thermovat chemical seasoning system.

During his many years as shop instructor in Wisconsin, Spielman published manuals, teaching guides, and more than 14 popular books, including *Modern Wood Technology*, a college text. He also wrote six educational series on wood technology, tool use, processing techniques, design, and wood-product planning.

Author of the best-selling *Router Handbook* (over 600,000 copies sold), Spielman has served as editorial consultant to a professional magazine, and his products, techniques, and many books have been featured in numerous periodicals.

This pioneer of new ideas and inventor of countless jigs, fixtures, and designs used throughout the world is a unique combination of expert woodworker and brilliant teacher—all of which have endeared him to his many readers and to his publisher.

At Spielmans Wood Works in the woods of northern Door Country, Wisconsin, he and his family create and sell some of the most durable and popular furniture products and designs available.

Bill Dehos is a wood artist whose work is widely acclaimed for its originality and quality. He is self-taught and has been carving professionally for the past twelve years. His keen understanding of nature has contributed to his sensitive interpretations of wildlife, which have won him such an enthusiastic following.

His work has been shown at exhibits and special showings at some of the best galleries in Door County, Wisconsin. He has received many commissions from prominent art lovers. Many of the works that appear here are on exhibition at the Spielmans Wood Works Gallery in Fish Creek, Wisconsin.

Mr. Dehos's first book, which was also coauthored by Patrick Spielman, was *Carving Large Birds* (New York: Sterling Publishing Co., Inc., 1986). This popular book on the subject of carving life-size large birds, a companion volume to this one, has attracted much attention to Mr. Dehos's work.

Should you wish to write Pat or Bill, please forward your letters to Sterling Publishing Company.

CHARLES NURNBERG
STERLING PUBLISHING COMPANY

CURRENT BOOKS BY PATRICK SPIELMAN

Alphabets and Designs for Wood Signs. 50 alphabet patterns, plans for many decorative designs, the latest on hand carving, routing, cutouts, and sandblasting. Pricing data. Photo gallery (4 pages in color) of wood signs by professionals from across the U.S. Over 200 illustrations. 128 pages.

Carving Large Birds. Spielman and renowned woodcarver Bill Dehos show how to carve a fascinating array of large birds. All of the tools and basic techniques that are used are discussed in depth, and hundreds of photos, illustrations, and patterns are provided for carving graceful swans, majestic eagles, comical-looking penguins, a variety of owls, and scores of other birds. Oversized. 16 pages in full color. 192 pages.

Gluing & Clamping. A thorough, up-to-date examination of one of the most critical steps in woodworking. Spielman explores the features of every type of glue—from traditional animal-hide glues to the newest epoxies—the clamps and tools needed, the bonding properties of different wood species, safety tips, and all techniques from edge-to-edge and end-to-end gluing to applying plastic laminates. Also included is a glossary of terms. Over 500 illustrations. 256 pages.

Making Country-Rustic Furniture. Hundreds of photos, patterns, and detailed scaled drawings reveal construction methods, woodworking techniques, and Spielman's professional secrets for making indoor and outdoor furniture in the distinctly attractive Country-Rustic style. Covered are all aspects of furniture making from choosing the best wood for the job to texturing smooth boards. Among the dozens of projects are mailboxes, cabinets, shelves, coffee tables, weather vanes, doors, panelling, plant stands and many other durable and economical pieces. 400 illustrations. 4 pages in full color. 164 pages.

Making Wood Decoys. A clear step-by-step approach to the basics of decoy carving. This book is abundantly illustrated with closeup photos for designing, selecting, and obtaining woods; tools; feather detailing; painting; and finishing of decorative and working decoys. Six different professional decoy artists are featured. Photo gallery (4 pages in full color) along with numerous detailed plans for various popular decoys. 160 pages.

Making Wood Signs. Designing, selecting woods and tools, and every process through finishing are clearly covered. Hand-carved, power-carved, routed, and sandblasted processes in small to huge signs are presented. Foolproof guides for professional letters and ornaments. Hundreds of photos (4 pages in full color). Lists sources for supplies and special tooling. 144 pages.

Realistic Decoys. Spielman and master carver Keith Bridenhagen reveal their successful techniques for carving, feather-texturing, painting, and finishing wood decoys. Details that you can't find elsewhere—anatomy, attitudes, markings, and the easy step-by-step approach to perfect delicate procedures—make this book invaluable. Includes listings for contests, shows, and sources of tools and supplies. 274 closeup photos, 28 in color. 224 pages.

Router Handbook. With nearly 600 illustrations of every conceivable bit, attachment, jig, and fixture, plus every possible operation, this definitive guide has revolutionized router applications. It begins with safety and maintenance tips, then forges ahead into all aspects of dovetailing, free-handing, advanced duplication, and more. Details for over 50 projects are included. 224 pages.

Router Jigs & Techniques. A practical encyclopedia of information, covering the latest equipment to use with your router, it describes all the newest of commercial routing machines, along with jigs, bits, and other aids and devices. The book not only provides invaluable tips on how to determine the router and bits best suited to your needs, but tells you how to get the most out of your equipment once it is bought. Over 800 photos and illustrations. 384 pages.

Scroll Saw Handbook. This companion volume to *Scroll Saw Pattern Book* covers the essentials of this versatile tool, including the basics (how scroll saws work, blades to use, etc.) and the advantages and disadvantages of the general types and specific brand-name models available on the market. All cutting techniques are detailed, including compound and bevel sawing, making inlays, reliefs, and recesses, cutting metals and other non-woods, and marquetry. There's even a section on transferring patterns to wood! Over 500 illustrations. 256 pages.

Scroll Saw Pattern Book. This companion book to *Scroll Saw Handbook* contains over 450 workable patterns for making wall plaques, refrigerator magnets, candle holders, pegboards, jewelry, ornaments, shelves, brackets, picture frames, signboards, and many more projects. Beginners and experienced scroll saw users alike will find something to intrigue and challenge them. 256 pages.

Scroll Saw Puzzle Patterns. 80 full-size patterns for jigsaw puzzles, standup puzzles and inlay puzzles. With meticulous attention to detail, Spielman provides instruction and step-by-step photos, along with tips on tools and wood selections, for making standup puzzles in the shape of dinosaurs, camels, hippopotamuses, alligators—even a family of elephants! Inlay puzzle patterns include basic shapes, numbers, an accurate piece-together map of the United States and a host of other colorful educational and enjoyable games for children. 8 pages of color. 256 pages.

Working Green Wood with PEG. Covers every process for making beautiful, inexpensive projects from green wood without cracking, splitting, or warping. Hundreds of clear photos and drawings show every step from obtaining the raw wood through shaping, treating, and finishing your PEG-treated projects. 175 unusual project ideas. Lists supply sources. 160 pages.

Index

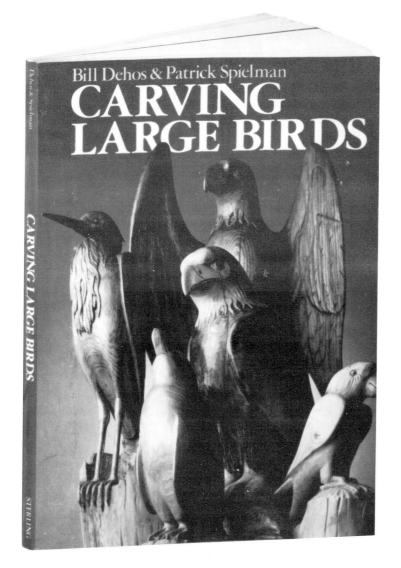